THROUGH MANY DANGERS

BRIAN H. EDWARDS

THROUGH MANY
DANGERS

POST OFFICE BOX 5, WELWYN, HERTS, ENGLAND AL6 9NU
POST OFFICE BOX 2453, GRAND RAPIDS, MICHIGAN 49501, U.S.A.

Paper ISBN 0.85234.069.9
Cloth ISBN 0.85234.075.3

ACKNOWLEDGMENT

Among the libraries and museums that have offered valuable
assistance in the preparation of this book, the author and artist
would like to acknowledge the Cowper and Newton Museum at
Olney, the Merseyside Museum and Liverpool Central Library,
the Rochester Public Museum in Kent, the Guildhall Library in
the City of London, the Manuscript Department of the Public
Records Office, the National Maritime Museum at Greenwich,
and in particular Mr Dennis Winston at the School of Oriental
and African Studies, and the Librarian of the Evangelical Library,
Mr Gordon Sayer.

Line drawings by Ken Reynolds
Cover design by Peter Wagstaff

Printed in Great Britain by
Stanley L. Hunt (Printers) Ltd., Rushden, Northamptonshire

CONTENTS

CHAPTER 1

THE ROAD FROM PLYMOUTH

The young midshipman strode briskly along the road to Torbay. As the noise of Plymouth receded and the sun settled below the ridge behind him he pulled up the collar of his jacket against the chill of the late spring evening. Every hour his step and heart became more confident; by the following mid-day he should have covered the thirty miles that separated *H.M.S. Harwich* from an interview with his father. Over and over he rehearsed his story; if only it would sound plausible to any dragoon he might chance to meet on the road. Behind him, on the man-of-war riding at anchor off Plymouth harbour, a furious Captain Philip Carteret raged at the desertion of his young officer; in front of him, at Torbay, a coldly severe father was fretting over the recent loss of some shipping in which he held an interest, ignorant of his son's proposed meeting. On the dirty road, John Newton, spattered with spring mud, was alone. But that was the story of his life. Since his mother died when he was just seven years old he had known few friends and had contrived to antagonise most with whom he came into contact, especially those in authority. Newton slept under the chill sky for the first night and set off early on his second day. As he shortened the distance to Torbay, he reflected on his nineteen years of life, laid plans for the future, and rehearsed his hastily concocted story.

CRADLED IN THE TRUTH

John was born in London on July 24th, 1725, but since his father was away at sea for most of his childhood, John's early upbringing was left to his mother. This frail, sweet-natured, God-fearing woman frequently drew her only child to her flowing skirt and taught him stories from the Bible. « She stored my memory, which was then very retentive, with many valuable pieces, chapters, and portions of Scripture, catechisms, hymns and poems. » Just ten years before Newton's birth, Isaac Watts had followed his *Hymns and Spiritual Songs* with a book of *Divine Songs for Children*. It was these songs that filled the house as mother and son worshipped together and prayed for the father who was away at sea. *Divine and Moral Songs* soon followed from the pen of Watts and with such themes as « against scoffing and calling names » and « against pride in clothes » Mrs. Newton found it valuable moral teaching with which to store the mind of her young son. Doubtless when he was a baby she would sing the beautiful lullaby that Watts, a lifelong bachelor, had included in his *Divine and Moral Songs*. This peace and loving warmth were shattered when John's mother died in 1732. She had longed for him to enter the ministry and to that end often commended him with many prayers and tears to God. It was a terrible day when his mother died, and even worse when his step-mother came into the home. He was treated well enough, but the new Mrs. Newton had little love for her step-son and less care for his soul. There were no more Bible stories, no more *Divine Songs* around the hearth, no more prayers before bed. John was allowed to mix with rough and profane children and he became hard, bitter and rebellious. A two years' stay at an inferior boarding school in Essex served only to hasten his indifference to religion; this was all the formal schooling he ever had.

At the age of eleven John was taken on his first voyage by his father, a captain in the Mediterranean trade. Captain Newton exercised a rigid discipline over his son and although the captain's cabin afforded refuge from the harsh life of the merchant service, his father was always severely distant. The sea air, coarse jesting and free living of the sailors made the young boy long to be a man himself—a real man, like his father's sailors. John made several voyages with his father, but at the age of fifteen was apprenticed to a friendly merchant in Alicante, Spain, « but my unsettled behaviour and impatience of restraint rendered that opportunity abortive ». Under the stern and rigid discipline of Captain Newton the spirit of the young boy was cowed, but away from his father his life knew few restraints.

His reckless decline was occasionally arrested, and Newton's life exhibited a conflict of conscience as he longed to rush thoughtlessly and lustfully into life but was checked by that fireside teaching at his mother's knee. Two incidents served to quicken his conscience; they were unremarkable in themselves but certainly used by an unseen hand to halt his flight from restraint. On one occasion, at the age of twelve, Newton was thrown from a horse and so narrowly escaped being impaled on the stakes of a newly cut hedge that for a while he thought seriously about Providence. On another occasion he missed, by five minutes, a trip in a longboat that was to take him and a friend to visit a man-of-war; the boat overturned and his friend was drowned. Newton was never able to swim (strangely, a very common lack amongst seamen in the days of sail) and the thought of brushing with death so closely sobered him for a while.

A POISONED MIND

As the midshipman now stepped out to Torbay such events seemed so trivial. He could laugh at them and tell them to the quarter-deck with elaborate details. They had no significance; he was just lucky. However, John could not escape the fact that at the time they affected him deeply. He could recall times when he determined upon periods of personal reform and « lived as a Pharisee ». In strange contrast to his normally cavalier life, he would spend long hours in reading the Bible, in meditation and in prayer. He fasted, once became a vegetarian for three months, and lived in constant fear of uttering an idle word. He was an ascetic but as he confessed years later, « it was a poor religion; it left me in many respects under the power of sin, and so far as it prevailed, only tended to make me gloomy, stupid, unsociable and useless ».   Such is the inability of man to change himself.   John admitted that he « loved sin, and was unwilling to forsake it ».   This malady, common to all men, led him into the depths of depravity before God Himself arrested the fall.

The young midshipman thought back to the day when he stumbled across a book that jolted him out of regard for his conscience.   It was a book that profoundly changed his thinking.

Lord Shaftesbury's *Characteristics of Men, Manners, Opinions, Times etc.* was first published in 1711 and by 1733 was so popular that a preface to the pocket edition claimed: « All the best judges are agreed that we never had any work in the English language so beautiful, so delightful, and so instructive... »   In essence the two lengthy and, to a modern reader, dull volumes contained a simple message.   The universe is ruled by a kind and benevolent mind and thus man should live benevolently also.   Human nature does not err: « when she seems most ignorant or perverse in her productions, I assert her even then as wise and provident as in her goodliest works ».   Deformity in the soul (what John had been taught to call sin) is due only to our « frail bodies and pervertible organs ».   Misconduct is nothing more than a bad taste in morals.   This, together with the earl's parody of religious zealots as « starched and gruff gentlemen », appealed to the rebellious spirit of the teenage Newton.   Shaftesbury was careful not to deny the Christian faith or a belief in God, and Newton had no desire, at present, to go that far; he considered the author « a most religious person », but his lordship's God was distant, impersonal and uninvolved in the affairs of the world and this was far more to John's liking.

With the evangelical doctrine of original sin and the consequent belief in a natural bias to sin locked within every man eloquently trampled upon, and with man portrayed as essentially good and virtuous, John could now wriggle free from the puritan theology of his mother. He learnt, by heart, whole passages from the *Rhapsody* in volume 2, and doubtless could recite in justification for his actions: « I shall no longer resist the passion growing in me for things of a natural kind, where neither art nor the conceit or caprice of man has spoiled their genuine order by breaking in upon that primitive state ». That opened the door to anything. Morality was for John Newton to make; was he not told that each man is to reason « what his good is and what his ill »? He considered that at last he had found the way to be truly happy. Thus with « fine words and fair speeches » his simple heart was beguiled. He read and re-read the *Rhapsody*, as he later confessed, until the slow poison trickled into the stream of his mind.

FOR THE SAKE OF MARY

John Newton felt strangely cold at the thought of meeting his father at the end of this road from Plymouth. Such interviews were always chilly affairs. He had tried his father's patience more than once. By the end of 1742 Captain Newton, despairing of his wayward son, had arranged to settle him in

Jamaica where young men were urgently needed to manage the plantations. A friendly merchant in Liverpool, Joseph Manesty, made the arrangements; the son, with the prospect of wealth and a licence to live as he pleased, readily agreed and the father, with the prospect of ridding himself of a troublesome son, was more than content. With a week to kill before leaving for Liverpool John decided to combine a small business trip for his father, near Maidstone, with a visit to a family that had nursed his mother in her last days of consumption. He felt he ought at least to meet the people who until now had been no more than names to him. Accordingly, on December 12th he turned into the drive of the modest but comfortable home in the West Borough of Chatham and was welcomed as a long separated member of the family. Mr. and Mrs. Catlett had three older children: Jack was eleven years old and studying hard at Rochester Grammar School, Elizabeth was thirteen and Mary, or Polly as she was affectionately called, was within a month of fourteen. There were other children in the family, down to baby George. The moment the young seventeen year-old adventurer gazed upon Mary his heart was lost. More than twenty years later he wrote: « Almost at the first sight of this girl I felt an affection for her which never abated or lost its influence a single moment in my heart. In degree, it equalled all that the writers of romance have imagined; in duration it was unalterable ».

John had been so warmly received by the Catletts that he stayed longer than the three days intended. Mary always behaved in a most proper manner before him and gave him little encouragement to think that his ardent love was in any degree returned. At first John was not sure what had overtaken him: « I was uneasy when you were absent, yet when you were present I scarcely durst look at you ». If he tried to speak he became confused but could not bear to leave her presence. Poor John! In a letter to Mary, many years later, he confessed: « My love made me stupid at first ». However, she clearly enjoyed his company and the three days became three weeks, which meant that he spent Christmas with Mary. The coach to London, and from London to Liverpool, had left and returned many times; the ship from Liverpool to Jamaica had sailed without him. John decided he would not, could not, go to the West Indies and be away from « Polly » for five years. When he finally returned to London and appeased the wrath of his father, John dared not give the true reason for his delay, in fact he could tell no-one of his love, not even the object herself. « It remained as a dark fire locked up in my breast. »

Mary was the only person alive whom he loved, for whom he would gladly endure anything and everything. It was for her that he so desperately needed an interview with his father. If only Polly could be his; he would suffer anything for the sake of his idol. The very thought of Mary quickened John's step on the road from Plymouth.

The clatter of hoofs, an oath, the jangling of harness, and midshipman Newton was back on the road to Torbay. Too suddenly for him to avoid their attention, a party of dragoons rounded a turn in the road and the young sailor found himself blurting out a

16

poorly constructed reason for his presence on the road without horse, pack or sealed orders, and with his back to His Majesty's fleet. The officer in charge could neither be fooled nor persuaded and the weary deserter, just two hours from his destination, trudged his way back to Plymouth. Manhandled like a common criminal through the town, Newton was hustled past the taverns and the drinking, grinning sailors, and into the small prison house.

For two days he was left here alone, to think. His first thoughts were not encouraging. John Newton had been aboard a man-of-war long enough to know what he could expect. A court martial and hanging at the yard would be merciful; but few were deliberately killed as man power was too scarce and war with France was imminent. Perhaps it would be a « flogging round the fleet »? Tied to the capstan he would be given twenty-five or thirty lashes across his bare back and then taken to each ship in turn for the same treatment until he had covered the whole fleet at anchor; the fact that a number of ships had been lost a few days earlier in severe storms was small comfort. Had he not heard that after such severe punishment « they almost always die »? To run the gauntlet would be less dangerous. The ship's company would be lined round the deck and Newton, stripped to the waist, would then be made to walk along the line, each sailor beating him with a length of rope with the master-at-arms walking backwards in front of him with drawn sword to slow the pace. Compared with this, to be « keel-hauled », dragged underwater from one side of the ship to the other, was a comforting thought. John could find no comfort in the *Rules of Discipline and Good Government to be Observed on Board His Majesty's Ships of War*, which were produced in 1730. Certainly they forbade a captain to inflict more than twelve lashes, but there were few punishments that actually amounted to less and when a hapless sailor « got a red-checked shirt at the gangway » and was dragged moaning and writhing below, who was going to report the captain? He was omnipotent on his own ship.

John had not long to dwell on such thoughts and after two days he was delivered to his commander and at once placed in irons. In these cramped quarters, restricted by space and shackles and deep in the bowels of the ship where the foul-smelling, stagnant filth of the ballast drove all purity from his nostrils and lungs, the recalcitrant sailor awaited his fate. It was not the first time that Midshipman Newton had aroused the anger of his commander, and Captain Carteret, R.N. determined that this would be the last. It was only by the intercession of the boy's father that he had advanced him to the quarter-deck and already he had overstayed his leave once and generally offended by his insolence and bawdy behaviour. Philip Carteret would now break his will and at the same time set a warning before the rest of his crew.

The entire crew was mustered on the main deck. The felon, stripped to the waist, stood on a grating where his feet, in the « stand-easy » position, were strapped down and his arms, spread out above his head, were fixed by the wrists. The marines were paraded on the poop, above and facing the sailors, to prevent any intervention by the crew. The ship's surgeon stood at one side, the master-at-arms at the other and everyone waited in silence for the punishment to begin. As the ship rose and fell with the movement of the sea, the breeze rattled through the rigging and the gulls mockingly screeched overhead, Captain Carteret, in full ceremonial dress, appeared from his cabin. Newton's crime, sentence, and the appropriate « articles of war » were read and

The offence was grave and the punishment fitted the crime.

the order given to commence. A boatswain's mate stepped forward and with a powerful arm and brutal rope lash flayed the white flesh from the prisoner's back. How many dozens, each by a different boatswain's mate, were laid upon John Newton is not recorded but although this captain was, by the standards of the day, « in general a humane man who behaved very well to the ship's company », the offence was grave and the punishment must have adequately fitted the crime. On an order from the captain the lacerated body was released, wrapped in a blanket and carried below. The surgeon performed the agonising ritual of cauterising the wounds with vinegar, neat spirits, salt water or hot tar, and the ship's company was stood-down to get on with duties.

A COMMON SAILOR

For days Newton alternated between consciousness and coma as fever racked his body. He was reduced from the quarter-deck to a common sailor and his former officer friends were forbidden to speak to him. Once more he was alone and friendless. Only his iron constitution and passion to see Mary enabled him to regain strength. He had failed in his bid to reach Mary but « I was willing to be or to do anything which might accomplish my wishes at some future time ».

In his miserable plight below deck, and before the ship's surgeon pronounced him fit to return to normal duties, John could return to his reflection on his life, a reflection savagely interrupted by those dragoons on the road from Plymouth. When John had failed to embark on the Liverpool ship bound for Jamaica, Captain Newton had lost no time in making alternative arrangements for his son, and John soon found himself serving as a sailor on board a merchant vessel working between England and the Continent. Thirty years after Newton first went to sea, Dr Johnson, the great essayist, historian and lexicographer, claimed: « No man will be a sailor who had contrivance enough to get himself into jail; for being in a ship is being in a jail, with the chance of being drowned. A man in a jail has more room, better food and commonly better company ». Life on board in the eighteenth century was cramped, disease-ridden and dissolute and it was well-nigh impossible for the seventeen year old boy to withstand the temptations and opportunities that surrounded him. Besides, there was no place for an ascetic, or an individual, in the community existence of the merchant vessel and, on his own confession, it was not long before John Newton had sunk with the bad example and bad company around him. He made « a few faint efforts to stop » but succeeded only in « making large strides towards total apostasy from God ». His mother's instruction, the hymns of Watts, the stories from the Bible, the vision of « Polly » and his own early efforts at self-reform could not arrest his fall.

It was during a visit to Venice, once the gateway to the East before the discovery of the Cape route to India, that Newton received a warning that he never doubted came from the hand of God; it was a unique experience in his life. He had a dream that was to prove a parable of his life. The scene was the harbour in Venice and Newton, on watch, was approached by a stranger who gave him a ring with the promise that while he kept it he would be happy and successful; the stranger added the warning that if he once parted with it he could expect only sorrow and misery. Newton, pleased with the gift, was soon approached by a second stranger who drew attention to the ring and ridiculed the promises made about it. Newton at first recoiled and then agreed to the suggestion that, to show his cavalier unconcern for such foolish promises, he should throw the ring into the water. At once the distant mountains burst into fire and the Alps became a terrible inferno. Reminded by his tempter that he had now forfeited all the promises of God, Newton saw the first stranger appear who, on learning the cause of his distress, recovered the ring from the water. The sailor advanced to receive the ring again, but the stranger withheld it saying: « If you should be entrusted with this ring again, you would very soon bring yourself into the same distress. You are not able to keep it, but I will preserve it for you. Whenever it is needful, I will produce it on your behalf ». This dream troubled him severely at the time and for two or three days he could hardly eat, sleep or continue with his duties. « But the impression soon wore off, and I totally forgot it. It hardly occurred to my mind again till several years afterward. » He continued with a life that he later described as one of « licentiousness and folly ».

If John Newton, tossing with pain in his hammock aboard the *Harwich,* and reflecting on his life, had stopped to assess the many occasions on which God had intervened in his life and had sown his mind with impressions of mercy upon his wayward life and careless walk, he could not but have sought the forgiveness of God in Christ. He had spurned all the promises and privileges held out to him. The cross, of which his mother had spoken so often, meant nothing to him; neither the love of a crucified Saviour nor the restraints of a holy God would change his life. The *Rhapsody* had set him free and free he would remain. It was only in later years that the converted prodigal realised the true state of his soul at this time: « I stood helpless and hopeless upon the brink of an awful eternity. Had the eyes of my mind been then opened, I should have seen my grand enemy, who had seduced me wilfully to renounce and cast away my religious professions, and to involve myself in complicated crimes ». In these later years too, he saw that just as his prodigal life had in reality not been freedom but slavery, so also the hand of a sovereign God had been marking out his path and preparing a place for repentance. « I should, perhaps, have seen likewise, that Jesus, whom I had persecuted and defied, rebuking the adversary, challenging me for His own, as a brand plucked out of the fire, and saying: « Deliver him from going down to the pit; I have found a ransom ». But Newton was to go closer to the pit before deliverance came.

THE PRESS GANG

Now a common sailor on the *Harwich*, John could only look back; after all, there was nothing to which he could look forward. Behind him was Mary, in front of him the prospect of five years' separation. John thought wistfully of his last meeting with Mary and the circumstances that brought him to the *Harwich*.

December 1743 had seen John once more home from the sea and making his way hastily to Chatham.

Unfortunately he presented a less attractive prospect for Mary. He might be able to excite young Jack with stories of the sea and impress the two girls by his « vast » experience and manly strength, but Mr. Catlett was of another mind. The young man was irresolute and disobedient, he had squandered the opportunity of a lucrative post in the West Indies and now was a common sailor occupying quarters « before the mast ». If he were an officer living abaft the main mast his pay would be poor enough, but a sailor was worthless. Although the awkward teenager had not yet proposed it, there could be no question of marriage. Once more Newton protracted his stay at Chatham, angered his father and this time paid dearly for his indolence.

In the early part of 1744 the French fleet was becoming increasingly aggressive in the Channel and George II grew alarmed. The shameful defeat of 1667, when the Dutch silenced the defenders at Sheerness, entered the Medway and attacked the fleet at Chatham, must never happen again. The King's new and energetic minister, Lord Carteret, ordered an immediate assertion of rule by the British squadrons. Recruitment was always a problem since there was no standing navy and losses by disease were enormous. The law allowed captains to send out « press-gangs » to help in the recruitment, and the merchant seaman was the prime target, (only the merchant captain, chief mate and pilot were protected by law). His bandy-legs, rolling gait and seaman's bawdy mouth betrayed him, but he would never willingly join the navy. The sailor's pay on a man-of-war was twenty-four shillings a month, but it was fifty

24

shillings in the merchant service and, as Daniel Defoe quaintly remarked in 1697: « who would serve his king and country and fight and be knocked on the head » for this differential?

Pressing was often expensive. By 1756 it could cost one hundred and fourteen pounds to impress one man when bounties had been paid; it was also ruthless, and gangs frequently fought each other for possession of a hapless victim. In 1796 an East Indiaman lay halfway up the Thames after completing a merchant run of many years; a naval captain, from *H.M.S. Britannia,* boarded the ship and in sight of wives and sweethearts impressed the entire crew. Only an outward bound ship was immune from the « press ». Impressment was one of the most cruel and barbaric customs ever imposed and to avoid it men would dismember their own fingers, fain paralysis or wipe nettles over their bodies to simulate a dreadful rash.

On Wednesday February 8th, 1744 the first lieutenant of *H.M.S. Harwich* made the following brief entry into his log: « I and 31 Men went on board the Bettsy Tender in order to Impress ». His orders were also to obtain supplies for the forthcoming voyage, and the Bettsy Tender slipped out of Harwich Harbour and by Sunday 12th was anchored off Sheerness in Kent. A week later Lieutenant Ruffin recorded that he had taken on « 15 Men from Chatham Hospital, 3 prest Men and 2 from Sheerness Hospital ».

On Saturday 25th, a day which, according to the captain's log, was one of strong gales and snow, John Newton was one of eight impressed men delivered on board *H.M.S. Harwich* together with the bread,

HMS Harwich a fourth-rate man-of-war.

brandy, beef, butter, pork, suet, peas, oatmeal, cheese and vinegar, not to detail the guns, tackle and two hundred and twenty barrels of powder that the first lieutenant delivered to his captain. *H.M.S. Harwich* was a fourth-rate man-of-war of nine hundred and seventy-six tons and fifty guns. The ship, built at Harwich in 1742, was originally called *Tiger* but renamed in November, 1743. Her captain was desperately in need of more hands to complete his crew, and, in a vessel whose gun deck measured one hundred and forty feet and whose beam was a bare forty feet, the cramped conditions of the crew of three hundred and fifty men are not hard to imagine. Of his new experience Newton commented briefly: « I endured much hardship for about a month ». If life was harsh in the merchant service, it was callous in the navy. For the first month Newton shared the diet of the other sailors: sea-cakes (hard flour and water made into a dough and usually alive with maggots after a few weeks at sea), salt-beef and salt-pork which was « neither fish nor flesh but savoured of both ». The meat was often so black and tough that sailors idled away their few leisure hours by carving it into models and polishing it. Cheeses were known to have been used as trucks to the ship's flagstaffs and they withstood the elements as bravely as the stoutest timber; frequently the sailors made buttons for their jackets and trousers from the cheese. A first hand description of the ship's biscuit claimed: « It was so light that when you tapped it on the table it fell almost into dust and there-out numerous insects called weevils crawled; they were bitter to the taste and a sure indication that the biscuit had lost its nutritious particles. If instead of these weevils, large maggots with black heads made their appear-

27

ance, then the biscuit was considered to be only in the first stage of decay; these maggots were fat and cold to the taste, but not bitter ». The water was invariably green and alive; no one understood the effects of bacteria. It was said of the seaman: « He hath an invincible stomach which, ostrich like, could well nigh digest iron ». It often had to. Pea soup was about the only item that the cook found it hard to spoil. Scurvy, from lack of Vitamin C, and dysentery, from the filth of the bilge over which the sailors lived and slept, took a heavy toll. It would be another fifty-one years before the Admiralty ordered green food, fresh fruit and lemon juice as effective preventatives to scurvy. During the Seven Years' War from 1756-63 it was estimated that of the one hundred and eighty-five thousand men raised for sea service, over two-thirds died of disease. According to Lord Nelson, the useful life of the seaman ended at forty-five; by then, if still alive, he was racked by agues, distorted with rheumatism and crippled by rupture.

Fortunately for Newton, his father intervened and, though unable to procure his son's release during a period of war alert, he was able to secure his promotion to the quarter-deck where, as a midshipman, he was entitled to some command, « which, being haughty and vain, I had not been backward to exert ». He could now bully, order and treat with contempt those with whom he once gnawed at the inedible cheese and biscuits. Newton's closest friend on the quarter-deck was a young man « of exceedingly good natural talents »; he was a freethinker and did not find it hard to encourage the new arrival to complete the « liberating » process that the *Rhapsody* had begun. John idolized his friend and was bitterly saddened when, some months later, a violent storm carried him overboard, and swept him into eternity. He had listened to his friend's arguments and drunk in his words of « wisdom » until at last « I renounced the hopes and comforts of the Gospel, at the very time when every other comfort was about to fail me ».

No sooner had John been converted to this free-thinking than he turned apostle for the cause, and found a ready listener in a young and impressionable man called Job Lewis. Job idolized John almost as much as John idolized his older friend. In between the long hours of duty Newton was pleased to pass on to Job Lewis such gems as fell from the eloquent lips of his older friend; and to pass them on with that air of wise authority that implied they were his own. Newton started Lewis on the slippery path upon which he himself had embarked. The three friends laughed at the Bible, mocked true religion and bartered their souls for the world. Years later, when Newton tried desperately to arrest the fall of Job Lewis and reverse all that he had now imprinted upon his mind, he discovered how wild and humanly irreversible is this road.

In December, 1744, Newton obtained permission for a day's shore leave and at once took horse to Chatham. It was not an altogether successful meeting and Mary did not offer him much encouragement. He returned to his ship on New Year's day and felt pleased to be dismissed from the captain's cabin with a stern warning only. At this time John's spirit was full of despondency. He had little enough in this life, but had convinced himself that there was nothing to look forward to after death. It was only his burning love for Mary that kept a spark of hope alive in his heart. A letter addressed to Mary and written from the *Harwich* on January 24th, 1745, reveals his state at this time:

> « But for you, I had till this time remained heavy, sour, and unsociable. You raised me from the dull melancholy I had contracted, and pushed me into the world. It is now more than two years since, from which time till now I have been almost continually disappointed in whatever I have undertaken... »

Without God, he was without hope in the world.

CONVOY DUTY

H.M.S. Harwich left Spithead early in 1745 and John learned that the fleet was due to be sent on a commission that would certainly keep them from home for five years. The thought of the separation from Mary, unrequited as his love appeared to be, was unbearable, and when the fleet was forced into Plymouth by a fierce storm, Newton betrayed his trust, deserted a party of sailors he was sent ashore to guard and set out on the road to Torbay.

Tossing in his hammock, nursing his torn back, and cursing the dragoons who discovered him, John Newton could see nothing but unrelieved gloom in his life. His conscience tormented him more than his wounds. His mother, Mary, a wasted life, a rejected hope of salvation, all crowded his imagination. « My breast was filled with the most excruciating passions, eager desire, bitter rage, and black despair... Inward or outward I could perceive nothing but darkness and misery. »

When the *Harwich* finally left Plymouth, John gave up all hope of seeing Mary for many years. He watched the coast line disappear into the mists and for a moment contemplated throwing himself into the sea; only the thought of Mary's reaction restrained him. A sharp order jerked him back into reality; there was little time to gaze into the past or the future on board a man-of-war. The idle sailor would soon become indolent and insolent. Some captains would beat a sailor for no other offence than smiling in the presence of an officer and every officer carried canes and ropes as « starters » to enforce the immediate obedience of an order. It is little wonder that to survive (and it is amazing that so many did) the Jack Tar of the British Navy had to be a man of iron « able to carry a hundred-weight of pewter (lead shot) without stopping at least three miles ».

Convoy duty could usually be relied upon to provide some action, even if it was only by way of loyalty to the crown. The year before, on June 12th, the sailors stood to their guns and whilst the ship drifted aimlessly in the « light airs » the captain recorded: « Fired 17 guns it being His Majesty's Accession to the Throne. At 10, pressed 7 men from the *William* from Jamaica, sent a mate and six men in their room ». Newton watched the pressed men board the *Harwich* with an understanding sympathy. By June 20th, 1744, the guns were in action for another reason, and a French vessel

31

from Dunkirk, with a mixed cargo, 20 guns and one hundred and seventy six men on board was captured and sent, under escort, as a prize of war to England. On Sunday, September 30th the *Harwich* engaged a French warship, also from Dunkirk. Action commenced at six in the morning and by half past one the captain reported graphically: « Came up with her, gave her a Broadside from the Upper Decks and Tops. She returned her Broadside, Tacked and fired her other. At 7 came up with her again and gave her a Broadside with the Upper Decks and 7 of the Lower Deck guns. She gave us her Broadside and Handgrenades and fell astern ». By eight in the evening she had struck her colours. The British warship suffered one man wounded and a great deal of rigging and timber shot through. Newton enjoyed the action, the smell of smoke, the splintering of timber and the cries of battle; it was hard fought, with the enemy able to come close enough to discharge her grenades. John's blood ran fast in his veins. It was a far cry from the Sundays of Isaac Watts and Bible stories at his mother's knee.

However, convoy duty was not all action. Illness was rife among the sailors and by March 7th, 1745 the captain logged: « Sent 35 sick men on shore to the Hospital ». On the 27th he deemed it wise to « read the Articles of War to the Ship's Company »; perhaps the day of Newton's savage punishment. When the *Harwich* finally arrived off Madeira in April there followed weeks of routine labour with little to break the drudgery and boredom apart from the day the captain « served hooks and lines to the Ship's Company »! Otherwise the following entry from the commander's log for Saturday, May 11th could have been for any day: « Light breeze of wind. At 3 p.m. served slops to the Ship's Company. At 7 served the Ship's Company 3 pints of water with a pint of wine ». The tedious routine of the common sailor was aptly described by a second lieutenant James Loggie, in one day's entry: « Tarred the Guards, Scraped the Sloop's Sides, and stayed the main mast Upright and Let up the main Shrouds ».

John's only comfort during these tedious days, when the fury of forced separation raged in his heart, was to design the death of the captain, to be followed immediately by his own. This, so Newton thought, would end all his sorrow at once. But the secret hand of God forbade him carrying out such a drastic answer to the problems which John Newton alone had made, and which God, alone, could cure.

CHAPTER 2.

WEST AFRICAN SLAVERY

A midshipman swaggered through the lower deck, heaved his shoulder at the inert form still sleeping in his hammock and roared: « A sharp knife, a clear conscience and out or down is the word ». Then, a swift slash at the lanyard and sailor Newton crashed onto the hard wooden floor. Cursing and squinting in the sunlight Newton appeared on deck and paused to assess the men about their duties. He could hardly complain at his rude awakening for there were more severe penalties set aside for idle seamen; on many ships the last man to obey an order was automatically punished. Newton glanced round the harbour at Madeira and took in the ships of the squadron riding lazily at anchor. His attention was drawn to a small merchant ship lying close by and then towards two crew members from the *Harwich* loading their pitifully few possessions into a boat. At once John knew what was happening; an « exchange » was taking place.

A naval captain had the right to intercept any merchantman and take off members of the crew that would be particularly useful to him, providing he replaced them from his own complement. It was an easy way of gaining a much needed carpenter or ridding himself of a dull or weak sailor. The arrangement could be most hurtful to a merchant captain who was powerless to resist. However, this exchange system could work to the advantage of the trader. Five years later when Newton had command of his own ship and was anchored off Sierra Leone he was only too pleased to put four mutinous crew members on board *H.M.S. Surprize,* and take four sailors from the warship in « exchange ».

However, in the present circumstance Newton thought only of a way of escape. He ran across the deck and pleaded with the boatswain to delay the departure of the two men. He next urged the lieutenant to intercede with the captain with the purpose of securing his exchange in place of one of the men preparing to leave. The lieutenant, who had no reason to concede a favour to an insolent sailor who had often given him trouble, spoke to the captain. Captain Carteret was now only too pleased to rid himself of such a thorn among his crew, although, at Plymouth, he had refused to transfer the beaten sailor even at the request of the admiral. Within the hour John Newton found himself on the deck of the *Pegasus,* a small merchantman bound for West Africa. Thus, in 1745, the year that « Bonnie » Prince Charles, having failed in his attempt to claim the throne of England, eluded the red-coats and sailed « over the sea to Skye », John Newton, having failed in his attempt to reach his father and claim a bride, escaped from His Majesty's Navy and sailed across the Atlantic Ocean to Sierra Leone.

SIN WITH A HIGH HAND

As the *Harwich* drifted into the mists of history and, fifteen years later, onto the rocks of Cuba, John Newton took stock of his new situation. At last there was a possibility of gaining a better station in life, a station that could claim for him the hand of Mary. Certainly there was adventure on a man-of-war but little prospect for an impressed seaman who had been publicly flogged and demoted.

The *Pegasus* was outward bound for Sierra Leone and the adjacent parts of the West African coast. Her cargo was composed of an uninteresting assortment of lead, copper kettles, brass pans, iron ladles, basins, boilers, guns, gun powder, knives and other miscellaneous items. Carefully stowed in her hold was a grisly array of chains, shackles, neckcollars, leg and hand-cuffs and thumb-screws. The *Pegasus* was a slave trader. Part of her cargo was the « money » with which to purchase slaves from the local traders on the West African coast, and the other part was the means by which the slaves were kept in order during the second leg of the trade mission from Africa to the West Indies or South America; a journey often exceeding seven weeks. Here the slaves would be sold chiefly for work on the plantations. Having sold the slaves, the ship would on-load sugar, ginger, rum, pearls, cotton and other commodities eagerly awaited by the British consumer, and return home across the treacherous waters of the Atlantic Ocean. This completed the final leg of what became known as the Triangular Trade; from England to

Africa with articles for barter, from Africa to the West Indies with slaves, and from the West Indies to England with merchandise for the home market. John Newton was to become very familiar with this Triangular Trade. The triangular journey was unlikely to take much under two years to complete. Some slaves were, of course, brought back to England and by the middle of the century it was estimated that no fewer than twenty thousand black slaves resided in London alone.

But at present John Newton was largely ignorant of all this. He had never been on a slave-ship before and took a lively interest in everything about him. The sailors engaged in such an inhuman trade were little better than slaves themselves and, like Jack Tar of His Majesty's Navy, were cowed and beaten under the iron rule and absolute authority of the captain. They were a blasphemous, drunken, promiscuous crew, and what better company for the young free-thinker? On board the *Harwich* men could remember the serious youth who arrived during that bitterly cold day in February 1744, and even when Newton finally abandoned all pretence to sobriety he could never quite live down his past. But the present was different. No-one knew him or his past. He came on board as a man of the world and would soon educate these ignorant sailors into a philosophy to match their profligate living.

To John's surprise he discovered that his new captain was acquainted with his father and in consequence, for a while, entertained a lenient and kindly disposition towards him. Indeed, as Newton later admitted, he might have done well in this ship; he was strong, healthy, by no means an indifferent seaman, and the son of a respectable merchant captain. But Newton was under the control of his own views and an evil heart and, like the prodigal son, was venturing into a far country there to squander his life. It was not long before his foul mouth and ribald behaviour earned the censure of the captain and lost his good will. « I not only sinned with a high hand myself », he later confessed, « but made it my study to tempt and seduce others upon every occasion ». John was possessed of the doubtful gifts of ready wit and quick repartee. On some trifling account he composed a poem which, without mentioning the captain by name, ridiculed the captain and his ship; it was not long before the entire ship's company were singing their new hymn, interspersed with oaths and curses at appropriate parts. Years later Newton longed that this part of his career should be « buried in eternal silence ».

For six months John Newton continued as a member of the crew, detested by the captain and first mate and by the same token applauded by the sailors. As the ship traded up the West African coast, Newton took his share in herding the slaves into the ship's hold. The business was barbarous. The men slaves were shackled together and locked away in the hold. Here they were laid out « like books on a shelf ». With barely five feet of headroom between decks, even this space was divided by a wooden shelf so that the slaves, chained in pairs, could be stowed away in two tiers. Forty years later when Newton was writing in support of the abolition of the slave trade, he observed on this part of the trade: « I have known them so close, that the shelf would not, easily, contain one more. And I have known a white man sent down, among the men, to lay them in these rows to the greatest advantage, so that as little space as possible might be lost ». Newton's own hands had once rolled the living bodies into place. The whole object was to fill the ship, and a vessel of little more than one hundred tons could be packed with two-hundred and fifty slaves in its hold. The heat and stench were unbearable; fever and dysentery took a heavy toll of life and not infrequently the dead and living were found shackled together in the morn-ing. The movement of the ship, even in a slight swell, could cause intense suffering since no-one could move without the consent of his neighbour. The lot of the women and girls was as bad, if not worse. Newton wrote vividly of the prey being divided by the sailors « and only reserved till opportunity offers ». Unlike the men, they were allowed the freedom of the deck, but when taken on board naked, trembling, terrified, almost exhausted with cold, fatigue and hunger, « they are often exposed to the wanton rudeness of white savages ».

But at that time John Newton was one of those « white savages ». Engaged in this bestial trade « every gentle and humane disposition » was hardened, like steel, against all impressions of sensibility. Pro-vided they obeyed orders, many captains allowed their men to live as they pleased, and most sailors did just that. « These excesses », wrote Newton, « if they do not induce fevers, at least render the constitution less able to support them; and lewdness too frequently terminates in death. » When John Atkins, a surgeon in His Majesty's ships *Swallow* and *Weymouth*, visited these coasts in 1735 he complained of the appalling losses suffered at Sierra Leone due to the malignant fevers brought on by the wines, weather and women; losses so great that at one time neither ship had man power sufficient to weigh anchor, and the *Weymouth*, which brought two-hundred and forty men from England, recorded two-hundred and eighty « dead upon her Books » before the end of the voyage! In the month of July almost ten years later Newton was writing at sea to his wife and, referring to these days, he returned thanks for being delivered « from the most abandoned scenes of profligacy, when I was sunk into complacency with the vilest wretches ». Eternal silence must bury the detail.

FEVER

After six months with the *Pegasus*, Newton's situation changed once more. Just as the ship was ready to leave for the « Middle Passage » to the West Indies, the captain died and the first mate took command. John was under no illusions but that his behaviour had earned him such hatred from the mate that he would be exchanged on board the first man-of-war they encountered. This was a fate more dreadful than death. On the day the vessel sailed John Newton landed on the island of Benaroes and engaged himself to the service of a successful trader called Clow. He received no wages for his six months' service on the *Pegasus* and the bill upon the owners was never honoured, for the company went bankrupt before he returned to England. What John did not know was that he would receive no payment for his next year's service either! But with high hopes of success and quick riches the young man stepped ashore clutching one book in his hand and with little else other than the clothes upon his back, as if he had escaped a shipwreck.

Clow was one of the few Europeans trading inland for slaves and bringing them to the coast where they were sold for a good profit to the slave-ships. Although Britain had been trading with Africa since 1553, it was not until 1625 that English ships entered the slave market. Queen Elizabeth I was said to have been horrified at the thought of carrying off blacks against their consent, declaring: « It would be detestable, and call down the vengeance of Heaven upon the undertakers ». Sir John Hawkins, one of her greatest sea captains, promised to respect this nicety of conscience in his royal mistress, but the promise was short lived and the scruples soon forgotten; Sir John became one of those first « undertakers »!

By 1689 The Royal African Company had entered into a contract with the government of Charles II to supply slaves to the West Indies. At first few Englishmen meddled with the business much beyond the anchor of their own ship, but eventually white traders penetrated the interior to speed the transportation of slaves to the coast. These men were rich and lived in luxury, with as many wives, servants and vices as they cared to own. Clow was no exception. It was never his business actually to enslave a negro; the white men were sufficiently canny to arrange for the black man to enslave his own kind. Tribal chiefs would sell unwanted children or men who had offended the community by one crime or another. Man-stealing, or « panyarring » as it was called, was a common source of slaves. By this, any man could seize another, providing he could prove that the hapless victim had defrauded or cheated him. When the supply of slaves was insufficient, Clow would arrange tribal

A plentiful supply of slaves.

warfare, supplying one side with guns to ensure a quick victory. Thousands were slaughtered and thousands more enslaved. In this way many local black kings became potentates in their own realm and were courted and gifted by the white traders to ensure a plentiful supply of slaves. But all this was dangerous work and demanded hard living. In a land of swamps and fever, tribal wars and superstition, strong drink and a freedom to enjoy any vice at hand, and in a land where the white man was loved by a few for his trade and hated by most for his butchery, life was uncertain and frequently very short. At best it was « the pleasures of sin for a season ».

When Newton joined with Clow to share in this nefarious business, he trusted himself to the honesty of the experienced trader and no formal contract protected his service from abuse. Clow had recently moved to a new area for trading, a low sandy island about two miles in circumference and almost covered with palm trees. It was one of three small islands two miles from the mainland and close by the mouth of the Sherbro river; together they were called the Plantains, so named after the banana-like fruit that formed a staple item of food throughout the tropics. Clow and Newton were not the first settlers here, and it is possible that the infamous pirate John Leadstone, « old Captain Cracker », had erected a fort and slave compound here as early as 1720. Clow and Newton built their house and began work. They could trade with the interior using the Sherbro river, and then retreat to the island refuge with the newly acquired human cargo.

Newton might have achieved the success he longed for had it not been for the fact that Clow was greatly influenced by a black woman with whom he lived. She was a woman of some importance and had been largely instrumental in Clow's success. For some reason that John could never discover she took an instant dislike to the newcomer and soon found occasion to vent her hatred upon him. When Clow was ready to embark on a trading venture, John was overtaken by a violent fever and he was left in the hands of the black wife. P.I., as Newton ever after called her (for the simple reason that her name sounded like those two letters placed together) at first took some care over his condition, but since he did not improve she soon neglected him.

For days his fever burned and it was with difficulty that he could procure some cold water to quench his terrible thirst. His life hung loosely between recovery and death. In days of delirium, faces and scenes flashed across his mind: his mother and the fireside stories and hymns; his stern, unbending father as he made his apologies for over-staying at Chatham; Lieutenant Ruffin and the cruel handling from the press gang; the unbelieving leer of the dragoon officer; the threatening boom of Captain Carteret and the harsh lash of the boatswain's whip; the days of misery and moments of unbridled pleasure; but above all, Mary. What would Mary think if she could see him now? Lying on a filthy mat spread over a hard board, a log of wood roughly pushed under his head for a pillow, and slaves pitying his misery. John Newton received with the gratitude of a beggar the remains of P.I.'s meal handed to him on her plate.

One day his extreme weakness caused him to drop the plate of scraps offered him; as he watched his pathetic meal soak into the dust, P.I. merely laughed and refused to give him more. His growing hunger forced him to crawl out at night and pull up roots in the plantation at the risk of being punished as a thief. These roots, « as unfit to be eaten raw as a potato », he chewed with relish. P.I. made sport of

45

him during his slow recovery; she would force him to walk when he could barely rise from his bed. Her servants would be sent to mimic his feeble attempts, clap in mock applause as he staggered across the yard and throw limes or stones at his wasted frame. He became « the sport of slaves; or what's more wretched yet, their pity ».

Who could imagine that this abandoned pitiable specimen would one day befriend a national poet, correspond with the most successful playwright of the day, give counsel to an eloquent and popular minister of state and occupy the pulpit of the parish of the first magistrate of the capital city of the greatest nation in the world?

When Clow returned from his trading, John complained of his ill-treatment. Not only was he not believed but P.I. resented him all the more. Newton was fit enough to accompany his master on the second trading voyage up river and they worked together well and successfully until a fellow trader persuaded Clow that his assistant was dishonest and stole Clow's goods at night or when he was on shore. Newton was thus condemned without evidence on the charge of dishonesty which, with bitter irony, « was almost the only vice I could not be justly charged with ».

A PINT OF RICE AND A RAW FISH

From now on there was less pity for Newton than even P.I. had shown. Whenever Clow left the vessel, Newton was locked on deck with a pint of rice as his day's allowance. To supplement this meagre ration he was allowed to bait his hooks with the entrails of any fowls used at Clow's table. At slack water, in driving rain or burning sun, the ragged, gaunt slave could be seen standing on deck watching his line with eager longing. Any fish thus caught were devoured half-raw and half-burned and they afforded him a delicious meal.

Watching his line with eager longing.

August was part of the rainy season on this part of the African coast, and for weeks the heavy skies poured down an incessant hail of torrential rain. Rivers, rising more than twenty feet above their normal level, drained into the coast-land turning it into vast, impenetrable swamps and jungle. Mosquitoes bred in their millions, and the sky was thick with small flies carrying dysentery and death. The rains eased in September but by October, the « mouldy month », everything that had not been thoroughly dried was covered with a thick, stale mould. Sierra Leone was the heart of the white man's grave. John Newton, protected by nothing more than a shirt, a pair of trousers, a cotton handkerchief for a cap and a piece of cotton cloth about two yards long, was frequently exposed to these driving rains for twenty or forty hours at a time. The picture of this miserable wretch, sucking at a half-raw fish dipped in rice, huddled on the wind-swept deck, soaked by torrential rain and shaking in every limb, longing for the return of his master like a pathetic lap dog, is illustration enough of the « service and wages of sin ». At other times he was almost naked and his body was covered in blisters from the relentless burning of the sun; he had only to wake up in the morning, shake himself like a dog, and he was dressed. Nor was he any stranger to the gnawing pain of hunger and frequently had not « half a good meal in the course of a month ». This terrible ordeal broke his strong constitution and though he regained much of his strength, Newton found himself admitting almost half a century later that he could feel some faint returns of the violent pains he then contracted.

At the end of two months Clow and Newton returned to the Plantains. Newton's condition and treatment were unchanged but his spirit was almost broken, yet not to repentance. His resolution and will had been sapped and it was only the vision of Mary that gave him any meaning in life. Yet surely that must be a fading hope, a mere illusion. Even if she were still free, he had no right to claim her and, still less, the means to reach her. Apart from the clothes on his back he had but one possession in the world and, strangely, he would creep away to the beach when relief of duties allowed him and open his copy of Euclid's geometrical diagrams and theories and with a stick trace out the diagrams in the soft white sand. Without any assistance and with no purpose in view, John Newton, the servant of slaves, mastered the first six books of Euclid. Beyond this, he possessed nothing. His philosophy collapsed around him, the vigorous zeal of his young mind became dull and his spirit was humiliated and cowed. For a while he aped the primitive superstition of the natives around him and worshipped the moon! With an act of which even Shaftesbury would have been ashamed, Newton refused to sleep whilst the moon was visible above the horizon and thus worshipped the creature rather than the Creator. With a pathetic defiance he would maintain a semblance of decency by slipping quietly into the night to wash his shirt upon the rocks and, afterwards, putting it on so that it might dry by the warmth of his body while he slept. When a ship's boat visited the island John would hide in the woods to avoid the gaze of strangers. Cowed, but unconverted, « I was no further changed than a tiger tamed by hunger. Remove the occasion, and he will be as wild as ever ». In desperation he wrote letters to his father, explaining his plight but resolving not to return unless his father requested it. He wrote also to Mary, but had little expectation that his letters would reach her.

One day Newton was busy planting out some lime

49

TMD 4

trees. They were barely the size of a small bush and Clow and P.I. walked by and stopped to mock. « Who knows, » sneered the master, « but by the time these trees grow up and bear, you may go home to England, obtain the command of a ship, and return to reap the fruits of your labours? We see strange things sometimes happen ». With this stabbing sarcasm Clow continued on his way no more expecting the fulfilment of his prophecy than that Newton should become king of Poland. Within three years that foolish jest was literally fulfilled.

After a year of this cruel treatment Newton was able to gain Clow's permission to serve another trader and, in a career that had accustomed him to sudden changes of fortune, he was immediately clothed, well fed and trusted with the management of some thousands of pounds of his master's money and a factory on the Kittam river. Here, in company with another white man, he traded. Business flourished and his employer was well satisfied. At last John began to consider himself well contented with his lot. Like the other expatriates around him he could embrace the customs, even the religions, and certainly the pleasures of the natives themselves and within a short time, he, like them, would have little desire to return home. He would be a white man grown black.

In February 1747 the two traders were making preparation for a journey inland, but the late arrival of some necessary items delayed their departure. Newton was contemplating a duel with a local merchant who had offended him; he had prepared his pistols, appointed the place, and within a day or two was to back his challenge by action. He had already decided

50

it was to be a duel without quarter. John's companion walked idly on the beach, about a mile distant from the factory, when a vessel sailed past. The young man hurriedly sent up smoke as a signal for trade but the ship's captain was doubtful of the value of stopping here. It was not a usual place for trade and, besides, the wind was fair and the ship was already beyond the point. However, against his better judgement, the captain hove to and received the trader on board.

THE GREYHOUND

On the list of the company of merchants trading to Africa from Liverpool and licensed by an Act of Parliament in 1750 was the name of Joseph Manesty. A close friend of Captain Newton, he had already offered to settle the captain's son in Jamaica and was not a little annoyed at the young man's failure to arrive at Liverpool on the appointed day back in 1742. With the pressure of business he soon forgot the incident until he received a request from his old friend that should any of Manesty's captains discover John Newton on the coast of West Africa, Captain Newton would be much obliged if he would carry the young man home to England. At least some of John's pathetic letters had found their way home. When the *Greyhound* left England Manesty gave the master strict instructions to enquire after John Newton, and by a providence, unrecognised at the time by John, this very ship had been prevailed upon to drop anchor within a mile of Newton's factory and within hours of his proposed departure inland.

John's companion was received on board and at once the master asked if he knew of a man by the name of Newton. On hearing of his immediate presence the captain came ashore expecting to find a more than willing passenger for his ship. But the soul that is bound to Satan is too frequently like an ill-treated dog that will not leave its master even when liberty is offered. By now John was well-satisfied with his lot and was unwilling to exchange it. The master of the *Greyhound* was equally unwilling to lose his quarry and fabricated a story of a relative who had recently died and left John a bequest of four hundred pounds a year; for good measure the captain concluded that he had orders to redeem Newton from any debts, even to the amount of half his cargo. In addition the captain promised that John should share his cabin, dine at his own table and be his constant companion without any services expected in return. Though all these consi-derations should have prevailed strongly with him it was only « the remembrance of my loved one, the hope of seeing her, and the possibility that accepting this offer might once more put me in a way of gaining her hand » that finally decided the issue. And thus with what must surely have been a forlorn hope in his mind, John Newton boarded the *Greyhound* and within a few hours the scene of his ghastly slavery for the past fifteen months had disappeared from view.

The *Greyhound* was not trading for slaves, but for gold, ivory, dyer's-wood and beeswax. Sometimes the ivory tusk (« teeth » as the traders called them) weighed up to a hundred-weight each but elephants were more scarce than slaves. According to John Atkins the gold was obtained in the form of native images or fetishes moulded from gold, as lumps of rock-gold or, more laboriously, as dust-gold panned from mountain water-falls. A cargo of this nature took much longer to procure than slaves, and when Newton embarked on the *Greyhound* she had been trading along the coast for five months already and was to continue for another year, moving almost one thousand miles up the coast.

In spite of his incredible escape from slavery, the captain's hospitality, the progress homeward, and the thought of embracing Mary as his wife, Newton's mind showed no signs of change and his life of ease and comfort led him into a course of terrible impiety and profaneness. He later recorded sadly: « I know not that I have ever since met so daring a blasphemer. Not content with common oaths and imprecations, I daily invented new ones ». He was frequently reproved by the captain who himself had hardly gained a reputation for bridling his tongue! Newton was no drunkard and his father had often been heard to comment that whilst this remained true there was hope for his recovery. However, « for the sake of a frolic », John would promote a drinking bout and delight at the antics of those he filled with the cheap palm-wines of the African coast. One evening when the rest of the crew had turned in, Newton arranged, at his own expense, a drinking bout with three or four friends. The ship was anchored in the River Gabon; the night was clear and the water calm. A large sea-shell took the place of a glass and the group drank alternately rum and geneva (a Dutch gin which at that time was very cheap). Newton commenced and uttered some foul imprecation against the man who moved first from his seat, an oath which in the event was directed against himself. Ill-fitted for such a contest, his brain was soon fired and he leapt from his seat to commence a wild dance around the deck. Suddenly his hat dropped over the side of the ship and Newton lunged forward to jump into the ship's boat which, in his confused state, he considered to be right alongside. In reality the boat was at least twenty feet distant and had a companion not caught hold of his clothes as he balanced precariously on the rail, John must certainly have drowned in the still waters of the Gabon. He was so near to « sinking into eternity under the weight of my own curse », yet the evening's revelling continued without another thought of eternity.

At Cape Lopez a party of the sailors went ashore and, penetrating some woods, shot a wild cow and brought a portion of the animal on board. Towards evening Newton led the return to collect the rest of the carcass, but night enclosed them and they were soon hopelessly lost without lamp, food or weapons; one moment entangled in a dense forest and the next up to the waist in foul swamp water. Without star or compass and fearing the wild animals with which this forest abounded, the sorry group of men tramped around blindly, pitching into one swamp after another. It might well have been a parable of his life, but Newton was too busy cursing his luck and hacking his way forward to give room to such thoughts. Suddenly and unexpectedly the moon broke through the heavy clouds and confirmed that they were struggling deeper into the woods and away from the ship and safety. The weary and terrified party turned round and reached the vessel in a much exhausted, yet thankful, state.   The parable was complete.

Between the many adventures and riotous parties into which John threw himself with abandon, he would occasionally turn his mind to the geometry of Euclid; this was about the only serious thought he entertained in these long weeks and months.   With the one exception, of course, of Mary.   If ever the words of Paul to the church at Rome had a living example it was surely in the life of John Newton: he became futile in his thinking and his senseless mind was darkened.   Therefore he was given up in the lusts of his heart to impurity, to the dishonouring of his body, because he exchanged the truth for a lie and worshipped and served the creature rather than the Creator (Romans 1: 21, 24-25).   By the time the *Greyhound* was ready to leave Cape Lopez in January 1748 and set off on the long and dangerous journey of more than seven thousand miles across the Atlantic, John Newton's conscience had grown so weak that finally it ceased to operate at all.   He had been near to death on many occasions but had not the least concern about the consequences; his conscience no longer stabbed or pricked.   He could at last sin with a high hand and an untroubled mind.   « I seemed to have every mark of final impenitence and rejection; neither judgements nor mercies made the least impression on me. »

There was one fleeting exception to this.   John occasionally picked up a copy of Thomas a Kempis' « Imitation of Christ »; the book was lying in the captain's cabin and Newton read it with idle indifference. But on March 9th a sudden thought came to him:

« What if these things should be true? » The « Imitation of Christ » was written by a fifteenth century German monk, and by the time of Newton it was one of the best-known devotional books; it breathed a love and commitment to Christ. Momentarily John's conscience troubled him but the hardened sailor beat off these thoughts with the awful conclusion that he must now abide the consequences of his own choice.

As the *Greyhound* left the banks of Newfoundland on March lst and picked up the hard westerly winds that pushed her fast homeward, another chapter ended in the life of John Newton, a chapter that could be written without a mention of the name of God.

CHAPTER 3.

AN ATLANTIC STORM

March 10th, 1748, was a night of terror. The stiff westerly turned into a howling gale that ripped into the defenceless *Greyhound* with gusts of eighty miles an hour and tossed the tiny cork from crest to trough between thirty-foot walls of water. During the blackness of the night a heavy sea crashed onto the deck and slid below. Newton, washed from his bunk, staggered to the ladder with the cry of sailors in his ears that the ship was breaking up and sinking. He grasped the rail and hauled himself from the squelching cabin floor. Half-way up the ladder Newton met the captain who ordered him to return for a knife. John released his hold, dropped back to the floor and went in search of a blade. A seaman shouldered past Newton, clambered onto the deck and was immediately swept into a cold, choking grave. But John and the struggling crew had little leisure to acknowledge this horrifying death, for as the ship wallowed in the seas they anticipated the same fate at any moment. Cold, frightened and hopeless, the sailors went through those duties that stern discipline had instilled into them, in a desperate fight for survival.

The *Greyhound* was weak before she set out across the Atlantic. After two years on the African coast her canvas and cordage were thin and rotting and her hull was leaking. The shrinking timbers had been caulked with pitch and rope but the pounding seas had no respect for hard work and good intentions. On this terrible night the upper timbers on one side were torn away, the canvas ripped and masts and spars splintered. Despairing of efforts to control the ship, the crew ran to the pumps whilst others joined in with the defiant gesture of bailing out with buckets! The battered vessel settled so low in the water that it was virtually only her cargo of beeswax and wood that kept her afloat.

« THE LORD HAVE MERCY »

Within an hour of the first shattering wave, the dawn broke and the wind abated. The dozen men on board stripped off their shirts, tore up the bedding and began to plug the many holes through which the sea was pouring in its relentless effort to settle this mer-chantman for ever on the bed of the Atlantic. Newton was little affected. As he nailed some rough timber over his shirt to fill a hole he coarsely joked to a sailor that this experience would soon serve as a conversation piece over a glass of wine. The sailor's eyes filled with tears and he responded: « No, it is too late now ». Too late now! Strangely John's stomach turned over at these words but he fought off troubling thoughts as firmly as the crew fought off the ocean. At nine in the morning, spent with cold and fatigue,

58

Newton went to speak with the captain. As he moved across the crazy remains of a ship's deck he found himself uttering a first prayer since childhood: « If this will not do, the Lord have mercy on us ». The sin-stained seaman clamped his mouth shut. What had he to do with peace or mercy? What right had he to call upon God or to expect a reply? Newton made his way uneasily to the pumps where, lashed down against every wave that still persisted in passing over rather than under the vessel, he worked until mid-day. But no longer could he be brash in face of his impending death. The uncouth ribaldry would not come; the easy banter, to assure the others there was nothing to fear, refused to flow off his tongue. If the Scriptures were true, he considered with despair, then John Newton for one could expect no mercy. For ten days the stricken *Greyhound* wallowed in the troughs of the Atlantic whilst Newton wallowed miserably in the depths of bitter resentment and utter despair.

March 21st was a day that Newton never allowed to pass unnoticed throughout the remainder of his life for, in his own words: « On that day the Lord sent from on high and delivered me out of deep waters ». On that day he worked at the pump from three in the morning until mid-day; then, for one hour, he was allowed the respite of his sodden bunk, into which he fell caring little whether he ever rose again. At one o'clock, being too exhausted to pump, he was lashed to the helm and, apart from one short break for some food, he continued here until midnight.

TIME TO THINK

His feet braced against the deck, his body roped to the wheel and his strong arms holding the ship as nearly on course as possible, John had time to

Time to think.

think. But it was not pleasant reviewing his life under the searching light of the Word of God. With nothing but the vast expanse of ocean around him John could pick out in his mind the stupid and reckless atheism that had ruined his past life like the broken and crushed deck of the *Greyhound*. Allowing the Scriptures to be true, he thought, there could hardly

60

be a greater sinner than himself. When he considered his debauchery and profanity, how often he had made the gospel a butt for his coarse songs, John was sure he had passed the day of forgiveness. These awful recollections seemed confirmed by the Scripture. His mother had impressed the Word of God into his mind and, such is the value of childhood instruction, nothing of his subsequent wild career had been able to erase many Scriptures from his memory.

As the cruel seas poured onto the ship and John shivered in his shirtless prison at the helm, verses of Scripture flashed into his mind and lit up his soul with the clarity and brilliance of the lightning across the ocean. Involuntarily he repeated Proverbs 1: 24-31 and his memory seemed divinely aided as he muttered above the wind and flapping canvas these condemning words: « Because I have called, and ye refused; I have stretched out my hand, and no man regarded; but ye have set at nought all my counsel, and would none of my reproof: I also will laugh at your calamity; I will mock when your fear cometh; when your fear cometh as desolation, and your destruction cometh as a whirlwind; when distress and anguish cometh upon you. Then shall they call upon me, but I will not answer; they shall seek me early, but they shall not find me: for that they hated knowledge, and did not choose the fear of the Lord: they would none of my counsel: they despised all my reproof. Therefore shall they eat of the fruit of their own way, and be filled with their own devices. » How accurately this suited his case. Had he not thrown off the counsel of God? And did it not seem that the Almighty was laughing at his despair? But Hebrews 6: 4-6 and 2

Peter 2: 20 appeared as ghastly spectres to hammer the last nails of judgement into his watery coffin: « For if after they have escaped the pollutions of the world through the knowledge of the Lord and Saviour Jesus Christ, they are again entangled therein, and overcome, the latter end is worse with them than the beginning ». How often the instruction of his mother, the *Divine Songs* of Watts and the visits of the dissenting minister at Stepney had impressed upon him the hope and assurance of salvation that could be found only in the cross of Christ. But he had squandered and then rejected the sturdy evangelical teaching of his childhood and had been entangled and finally overcome by the pollutions of the world. A black cloud of despair engulfed him and he felt himself « sinking under the weight of all my sins into the ocean, and into eternity ».

About six the following evening the ship was freed from water and the crew gained a little hope. John thought he could see the hand of God in this but was cautious; after all, his estimate of Providence had only a few hours' experience behind it. In the next few days as the broken vessel ploughed her way defiantly across the Atlantic, the shivering, aching sailors rationed the food and dared to entertain thoughts of land; and John Newton went on thinking.

From his black, unfathomable despair John turned his thoughts to Christ, a new venture for him. He recollected Christ's life and death: « A death for sins not His own, but for those who in their distress should put their trust in Him ». But he wanted evidence. The comfortless principles of infidelity were deeply ingrained and he longed to know that the

Gospel was fact and not fiction. John procured a New Testament and resolved to examine it more carefully. To profess faith in Christ when he did not even believe the historical truth of the gospel story he rightly judged to be a mockery of God. He thumbed the gospels and came upon Luke 11: 13: « If ye then, being evil, know how to give good gifts unto your children; how much more shall your heavenly Father give the Holy Spirit to them that ask him? » If the Scriptures are true, he reasoned, then this passage is true and that Spirit could aid him in his search for peace and assurance.

AN ANCIENT MARINER

The wind moderated and the ship drove on towards home. But the plight of the crew was still desperate. All the casks of provisions had been beaten to pieces and the livestock, pigs, sheep and poultry, had been washed overboard. A little coarse meal, intended for the pigs, was available; a little bread, some salted cod, fished from those banks off Newfoundland, and a pint of brandy made up the rest of their subsistence.

The next four or five days saw the little ship limping on; the sails had been largely torn away and now, even in a good wind, there was little canvas to be filled and the journey home was painfully slow. Suddenly, one morning, a cry from the watch tumbled the crew onto the deck and a chorus of voices hailed the distant land. It was a beautiful dawn and the sun, just commencing its long climb heavenward, silhouetted the outline of hills against a flaming sky. The near-beaten sailors congratulated each other as one by one they authoritatively identified the north-west coast of Ireland. On the captain's orders the remaining pint of brandy was shared among the celebrating mariners and the last slices of bread were hungrily consumed. Soon there would be brandy and bread enough. The ship, with new heart, rose and dipped to meet the land and the sun climbed higher above the horizon. But as it did so, the festivity waned, the mate growled an oath and the solid land puffed into the sky in deceptive balls of cloud. With a sickening realisation of their hasty joy and prodigal use of the last stock of food, the crew watched their hope evaporate into the distant sky. Within half an hour they were alone, once more, on the ocean.

For a week the sickly crew continued in their floating prison and a sailor died of exposure. The battered ship was forced to keep her broken side to the kindest weather, which meant that a change of wind drove her north of Ireland and far west of the western islands of Scotland. There was little hope of meeting another vessel in these waters and Newton fairly concluded that they were likely to have been the first ship to be in that part of the ocean at that season of the year. It could well have been this very sailor that Coleridge had in mind when he wrote the tragic *Rime of the Ancient Mariner* and included the lines:

> The fair breeze blew, the white foam flew,
> The furrow followed free.
> We were the first that ever burst
> Into that silent sea.

If the « Ancient Mariner » ran foul of the crew for shooting an Albatross, Newton had his troubles also. The Captain was soured by the disaster and incessantly reproached John Newton as the cause of all the distress. He was confident that, like Jonah, if Newton was thrown overboard they could all be preserved from death, and not otherwise. He did not intend to make this experiment, but the continual rehearsal in John's presence caused him an understandable uneasiness, « especially as my conscience seconded his words ». This ancient mariner had no doubt who was to blame for the present disaster.

The wind mercifully changed direction but the weather was bitterly cold, and with few clothes, little to eat and constant labour to keep the ship afloat, the crew took on the form of condemned men waiting only for the stroke of the executioner. But John Newton, after years of abandoned infidelity, had begun to pray and, as he later informed Mary: « My first, half-formed prayers were answered. He whom the winds and seas obey, in a manner little less than miraculous, brought me in safety to Ireland. » On April 8th, just four weeks after the storm and as the last food was boiling in the pot, the *Greyhound* struggled into Lough Swilly, one of the northernmost points of Ireland. Less than two hours after they had anchored in the comparative shelter of the bay, a gale blew at sea with such a force that the stricken ship would certainly have been broken to pieces; at the same time the sailors discovered that the six large water barrels, which they considered to be full and upon which they had staked their only hope of future survival, were, all but one, broken and empty. The stricken ship that

65

limped into the peace and safety of Lough Swilly became a picture of John Newton limping home to his God with many fears and doubts but believing at last that there is a God who hears and answers prayer. Such is the power of God to reverse the expectations of man that the tearful sailor who considered it « too late now » was soon laughing at his experience in the local tavern with a glass in his hand, whilst the most hardened, unimpressionable man on board was seriously reading the New Testament and a volume of printed sermons!

Whilst the *Greyhound* was refitting John went to Londonderry, a few miles distance, where he was received with all the warmth of hospitality that the inhabitants of this exposed coast traditionally afforded shipwrecked mariners. He attended church twice a day and prepared himself to receive Holy Communion. On that solemn day he pledged himself to live for ever in the service of God. This was no artificial religion hurriedly donned by a grateful survivor and as easily discarded; in all sincerity and simplicity John Newton renounced his sin and laid claim to the pardon that God has promised to give, « on account of the obedience and sufferings of Jesus Christ. By that time I embraced the sublime doctrine of God manifest in the flesh, reconciling the world to Himself ». The foul mouth and bawdy language became a thing of the past.

As a result of the warm hospitality offered by the inhabitants of Londonderry, John found himself, the day following that memorable communion service, invited to join a shooting party with the mayor. They trudged the moors and shot at the zig-zagging snipe, flushed from the tall grass. The party came to a small bank and John dropped his gun, trailing it at his side, to negotiate the mound more easily. Suddenly the heavy shooting piece fired and the shot flew so close to Newton's face that the corner of his hat was burnt away. His first communion was almost his last.

TO MARY AT LAST

Newton wrote to his father from Londonderry. The ship that carried him from the west coast of Africa had not been heard of for eighteen months and Captain Newton received the letter from his prodigal son, who was dead but now alive, just a few days before he sailed to take up the post of Governor of York Fort, in Hudson's Bay. Newton's father made plans for his son to join him in the near future, but although John made all haste to reach London in time, his father was compelled to sail without meeting his son and John had to be content with receiving two or three affectionate letters. Mr. Newton died tragically two years later while bathing and so never returned to England and his son was never afforded the opportunity of asking forgiveness for the pain he had caused his father. However, the old captain performed one last, undeserved but vital service for his repentant son. He visited Chatham and gave his personal consent to a union of John and Mary, should John pursue his love.

Healed of her wounds the *Greyhound* slipped into the Atlantic and, daring the ocean to follow her, turned east into the North Channel, down to the Irish

67

Sea and anchored in Liverpool harbour towards the end of May, about the very day that Captain Newton sailed out of the Thames estuary on his ill-fated commission to Hudson Bay.

Joseph Manesty, ignorant of being just eight years from bankruptcy, received John warmly and at once offered him the command of one of his merchant ships. Months earlier John would not have hesitated, but a new mind told him that he was as yet unfit for such a responsibility and he engaged to make a voyage as first mate. The mate of the *Greyhound* took command of a ship and this man became John's captain. But John had one urgent mission before the *Brownlow* sailed, and with all haste he made his way to Chatham. When John had arrived in Liverpool there had been no letter waiting him from Mary and with tears in his eyes he had written to her aunt expecting to hear that Mary was already engaged. The reply he received quickened his heart and his step; the door of hope was still open.

The Catletts received him warmly and John entertained hopes of a successful conclusion to his stay. But, for all his brash and reckless past, the presence of Mary melted him into a stupid and tongue-tied suitor. He was clumsy and awkward throughout the brief visit and felt he had achieved very little of his desire to communicate his love and purpose to Mary. In fact he succeeded only in gaining her permission to let him write to her!

Short of money, John walked back to his ship! He referred to it later as his « solitary walk to Liverpool »; it was as sad as it was solitary. He was annoyed with himself at not making his intentions more plain to Mary and despondent that he had so little to offer her. He dared not reveal to Mr. Catlett that he had no money for the return fare to Liverpool. After his return to Liverpool John wrote Mary a letter. If he was clumsy in speech he was eloquent with the pen. He waited impatiently for her reply, ready to smother his passion if he received an absolute refusal. But Mary, understanding more plainly his intentions, responded in a polite and proper manner, settling John's mind that she was free from any engagement and was not unwilling to wait the outcome of his projected voyage. As the *Brownlow* weighed anchor, John held that letter close to his heart. It was his passport to return.

AS BAD AS BEFORE

In God's economy of men, as England's greatest hymn writer, Dr. Isaac Watts, lay on his death bed in the beautiful Abney home at Cheshunt, another man, upon whose shoulders his mantle would fall, was being tossed upon the high seas in a cold uncomfortable vessel and with a new-found faith fighting for the mastery of his life.

If John had ever felt secure in his new-found faith, he was to learn by bitter experience on this voyage that the Christian, away from fellowship and teaching, is like a coal out of the fire. Soon after leaving Liverpool he grew slack in prayer and reading the Scriptures; his conversation became trivial, and by the time the ship reached Guinea John knew himself to be almost as bad as before. With the exception of profanity he fell an easy prey to all his old sins and « the enemy prepared a train of temptations... for about a month he lulled me asleep in a course of evil, of which a few months before I could not have supposed myself any longer capable ». His conscience troubled him at times and he resolved to return to the state of heart that had surrendered to the Lord in Londonderry. Like Samson he would say, « I will go forth, and shake myself, as at other times », but he was without strength, for the Lord seemed to have departed. But God did not leave him long in this miserable and helpless state.

Newton had now returned to the scene of his former slavery and his duty was to sail from place to place in the longboat to purchase slaves and deliver them to the *Brownlow*. The lime trees were within a year of fruiting and Clow and P.I. courted his trade. He was busy, successful now, and almost as careless of his soul as when he was last on this coast.

The longboat afforded little protection from the incessant rain. John was familiar with the aching limbs that resulted from being exposed in such a boat, five or six days together, without a dry thread about him. These boats seldom returned without bringing some of the crew dead or ill with fever or dysentery. The burning sun, as temperatures soared above one hundred degrees Fahrenheit (38° centigrade) during February, the rain and violent storms in a land that expected one hundred and fifty inches of rain each year, the long treks through tangled forests and mosquito-infested swamps, and the ever present threat of sudden or excruciating death at the hands of treacherous natives, all took a heavy toll of the white trader. First mate Newton buried six or seven members of his long-boat crew. It is therefore hardly surprising that he himself fell prey to a violent fever. During the long days of burning and shivering, when faces and voices swam around his giddy mind, John saw vividly his past prodigal life, the timely mercy of God in that Atlantic storm and his own ungrateful heart. Weak and almost delirious he crept from his bed to a secluded corner of the island and there threw himself upon the mercy of God. He made no great resolutions, but hoped and believed in a crucified Saviour. From that hour, not only did his health improve, but he was delivered from the power and dominion of sin. Not that he became perfect or ceased to battle against temptation, but never again did he fall into such a « black declension ».

Two years later John tried to explain to Mary why, after his first embrace of the gospel, he could fall so lamentably into his old ways. « I had some serious thoughts », he wrote, « was considerably reformed, but too well satisfied with my reformation. If I had any spiritual light, it was but as the first faint streaks of an early dawn. » In point of fact he had not been trusting wholly in Christ; he had still been trying to earn his salvation.

DROWNED IN HIS PLACE

No slaving voyage was uneventful and more than once his canoe, ferrying him from ship to shore, overturned and he was dragged from the surf more dead than alive. But one incident John found worthy of special note. The trade was finished, the ship was at Rio Cestors preparing to sail with her complement of two hundred and eighteen slaves. One of the mate's last duties in the longboat was to bring in wood and water for the voyage. Newton made several journeys, leaving the ship in the afternoon, spending the night ashore and returning with his cargo in the morning. One day John was preparing to leave as usual. He was actually sitting in the longboat, ready to cast off, when the captain appeared on deck and ordered him on board. John obeyed and reported to the captain expecting fresh orders. The godless captain gave no reason for his unexpected change of the invariable procedure, except that « he had taken it into his head », as he gruffly phrased it, to send another man in his place. That night the longboat, old and almost unfit for use, sank in the river and the man who substituted for Newton was drowned in his place.

The *Brownlow* left West Africa and sailed to Antigua in the West Indies and from there to Charles Town in South Carolina, by which time sixty two of the slaves had been buried at sea. When business allowed, John slipped away to the woods and fields to be alone with God, but the pull of sea-faring companionship drew him back to idle and worthless evenings. But more and more John felt himself drawn to the things of God. He employed his leisure hours on the long voyage home by revising his Latin, which he had all but forgotten, from extracts of Horace's *Odes* which he discovered in an old magazine. He wrote regularly to Mary and exchanged « sheet for sheet » with her brother. To Mary, John revealed little of the life around him, except to confess on one occasion that on board he felt shut up « with almost as many unclean creatures as Noah was and in a much smaller ark », but he was still « with an unbated passion and regard, your faithful admirer, and humble servant ». To Jack he described vividly the dangers at sea and on land.

When John Newton stepped ashore at Liverpool he despatched his official business as hastily as possible and set out for Kent. It was a wiser and spiritually stronger Newton who took coach to London than the one who had walked into the city eighteen months earlier. He was wiser for he had learnt important lessons in the school of suffering, and he was stronger for having been taught his own weakness.

Chapter 4

A NEW MASTER

The brief visit to Chatham passed pleasantly enough. The family listened to John's tales of the sea and Mary hung upon his every word. Jack was in London studying law and Elizabeth was no longer the giggling girl of his first visit seven years earlier. But the family, comfortably middle-class, respectably attending church, and profitably supplying the Parish Poor House with flour, bread, peas and other commodities, had nothing of the vital religion that John now possessed. John was a young Christian and had not yet talked with any minister or sat under any evangelical preaching, with the exception of a few sermons from a dissenting minister in Charles Town; John scarcely knew how to explain what had happened to him, let alone how to pass this treasure to others. Besides, he had other, pressing business on his mind.

At last, when John and Mary, with that unspoken communication of lovers, had contrived to be alone, the suitor trembled out his proposal. Mary was more positive; she too had waited, longing and hoping, and, with practical common sense, she was not going to allow this opportunity to pass. The beautiful young lady of twenty years accepted the proposition. In all his wildest dreams John had never actually planned for this moment. He had thought of it often, but it was always so unlikely, so far beyond his grasp; it had always been a castle built upon the ever evaporating clouds of his constantly changing circumstances. When it came, he sat stupid and senseless. The old clock on the wall ticked away solemnly and the two young lovers sat in awkward silence. A few years later John tried to explain his stupidity by writing an affectionate letter to Mary apologising for the embarrassment he caused her by his awkwardness: « My heart was so full, it beat and trembled to that degree, that I knew not how to get a word out ». The tongue-tied suitor just sat there, fidgetting nervously, until Mary broke the silence.

On February 1st, 1750, John Newton and Mary Catlett were married at St. Margaret's Parish Church in Rochester and settled with the family at Chatham. They could not afford a home of their own. It was true that the prospect of the command of a ship lay before him, but he had gained little from his last voyage and nothing from his long service before that. A small amount of money he had been expecting upon his marriage failed to materialise, so that John could honestly claim that, with the exception of their clothes, the sum total of his worldly inventory at the time of his marriage was « seventy pounds in debt ».

The early bliss of the young couple was rudely interrupted by an order that arrived in June offering John the command of a ship ready to sail to

Africa. John had been lulled by the peaceful life in West Borough and on his own admission rested in the gift and forgot the Giver. Leaving Mary in Chatham, John journeyed to his ship and on Saturday, August 11th, 1750, began his log with the entry, « cast from the pier head at Liverpool ».

The *Duke of Argyle* was a common « Snow » class merchantman, which was little more than a brig with nine sails and a displacement of just over one hundred tons. Her new master referred to her as « a very old and crazy vessel ».

The crew of twenty-seven besides the captain, first mate and surgeon, were the usual rough seamen who made up the work force of a slave-trading vessel. John knew them; they were all much the same and without stern discipline would soon take command of the commander. Of this crew, the first mate, surgeon, carpenter and four seamen were buried on the voyage, four were « exchanged » with crew members from *H.M.S. Surprize* and six were discharged. A ship rarely returned with the crew it took out.

The *Duke of Argyle* was stored with all those articles of trade that Newton had first discovered on board the *Pegasus* back in 1745. But now it was John himself who personally supervised the choice of shackles and collars for the human cargo.

TO MARY WITH LOVE

Once the ship was under way, the long and tedious journey had commenced, and the crew had settled into their routine, John had time to begin his regular and detailed correspondence with Mary. During the three journeys he made over the next four years, the young husband wrote over two hundred pages to his bride and, although some of them changed ships as many as six times in the course of their journey home, not one failed to arrive. He wrote two or three times a week, but a comparison of his letters to Mary with

His regular and detailed correspondence.

the details of his official log shows how careful he was not to alarm her with the dangers of his trade.

It was John's desire that in these letters they should assist each other in « the improvement of religion ». Mary thought he was suggesting that she was lacking in true religion (which she was!) and to this she strongly objected. John backed away a little, unwilling to offend the one he loved so much, but in July, just prior to his sailing, he returned to the issue: « If my dearest Mary will permit me to offer my best advice, and which I propose as a rule to myself—it is this—To endeavour to cast all your care upon Him, who has promised to care for us, if we will but put our trust in Him ».

In fact the letters of his first voyage contained little to reveal the deep state of his heart. He referred often to « Gracious Providence » and the « Great Deliverer » but as yet he was still learning the privilege of knowing that Gracious Providence as a personal, heavenly Father. Without doubt Mary was the idol of his life, and by September he admitted that he could find nothing deserving his attention « but religion and love ». He wrote long and beautiful love letters, expressing properly, and in fine language, the passion that he had for his young bride. « The only study now left me », John wrote on September 5th 1751, « is, how I may best deserve and requite your goodness. Good night. I am going to look at the north star ». John and Mary had agreed that at a certain hour each week they would look into the clear night sky towards the north star and in this way feel bound to each other across the thousands of miles of desolate water that separated them. Even this simple lover's act was a mark of his young faith. Looking back in later years he commented: « we knew but little then of the throne of Grace... at which all who love the Lord daily meet ».

The letters poured out their eulogies of a worshipping love.   Outward bound on September 18th John wrote: « I suppose that I am now about half way to Sierra Leone, and not less than fifteen hundred miles from my dearest—a great distance, and hourly increasing!   But it is not sufficient to divide you from my thoughts ».   A year later, homeward bound, he declared: « I owe to you the most that endears life to me ».   John ever felt unworthy of her love and was under no illusion as to the unattractiveness of his life and appearance.   In a letter written in April 1751 he jeered at himself by speaking of the reaction of Mary's acquaintances.   « How often must they have said— What!   the accomplished, easy, polite Miss C—, married to that awkward piece of formality, whose ridiculous behaviour was for years a standing jest among us! Strange! »   John's love for Mary was constant and faithful.   The letters continued during his second voyage—« I think of you continually and pray for you almost hourly »—and into his third voyage.   After that, whenever they were separated, John's letters followed Mary wherever she was.   That love, which exceeded all that the romantics could ever write of, continued unabated until Mary's painful death over forty years later.   After that sad event he wrote of his love for Mary during these long sea voyages: « My attachment to my dearest was great, yea excessive, yea idolatrous!   It was so when it began.   I think no writer of romances ever imagined more than I realised.   It was so when I married.   She was to me precisely (how can I write it?) in the place of God.   In all places and companies, my thoughts were full of her.   I did everything for her sake, and if she was absent... I could take pleasure in nothing ».

CAPTAIN NEWTON

The merchant captain, no less than the naval commander, had absolute power on board. John described his kingdom to Mary on September 21st, 1751 : « Excepting the pain of your absence (which I hope I shall always feel when from you), I have little to disquiet me. My condition when aboard and even in Guinea, might be envied by multitudes who stay at home. I am as absolute in my small dominions (life and death excepted) as any potentate in Europe. If I say to one, Come, he comes; if to another, Go, he flies. If I order one person to do something, perhaps three or four will be ambitious of a share in the service. Not a man in the ship must eat his dinner till I please to give him leave; nay, nobody dares to say it is twelve or eight o'clock, in my hearing, till I think proper to say so first. There is a mighty bustle of attendance when I leave the ship, and a strict watch kept while I am absent, lest I should return unawares, and not be received in due form. And should I stay out till midnight, (which for that reason I never do without necessity) nobody must presume to shut their eyes till they have had the honour of seeing me again ».

That last consideration for his crew revealed Newton as a humane and fair captain. He would not allow « any arbitrary or oppressive laws to be valid in my peaceful kingdom » and would frequently pay the fine levied upon those crossing the equator for the first time, rather than see them ducked almost to death. The old established customs of the captain's authority, however, were necessary to maintain disci-

81

pline; without it the common sailors would be unmanageable. Newton, therefore, kept strict discipline, and not all would agree that he had little to disquiet him.

On November 1st, 1750, he logged: « Gave two of my gentlemen a good caning and put one in irons ». This gentleman stayed there for four days but later, remaining as aggressive as ever, he was handcuffed and stapled to the deck. Whether *H.M.S. Surprize* cured William Lees we shall never know. The master of the *Duke of Argyle* put four mutinous crew members on board the man-of-war *H.M.S. Surprize,* but he did not get a good bargain, for on the last day of 1750 he entered the following record: « Detected Will Lapworth, one I had from on board the *Surprize*, of breaking the lock of the stateroom scuttle and stealing brandy; put him in irons ». If the members of his own crew gave him trouble the negro slaves were more dangerous still. On May 26th, 1751, Newton discovered that twenty of them had broken their irons, and a few weeks later a rumour that the slaves had poisoned the fresh water set the ship in alarm. It was not all who would envy this life.

It is perhaps hard to understand John Newton, a man so indebted to the mercy of God, engaging in the soul-destroying slave trade. But in the middle of that century it was a respectable and profitable career, a « genteel occupation ». After all, Protestant ministers in the Southern States were rumoured to own sixty five thousand slaves, and some years later the Bishop of Falk alone possessed four hundred. Few thought it incongruous that when Newton ventured upon the trade he should solicit the prayers of Christian people for a successful voyage, or that he should pen into the front of his log, « Laus Deo »: a journal of a voyage « intended by God's permission ».   John admitted that his conscience troubled him at times and he longed to be in a more humane calling with less to do

A genteel occupation.

with chains and shackles and thumb-screws, but as he stood on deck, arms folded, cutlass in his waist band and pistol to hand, it was the only life this Christian captain knew.

After their long journey through the forests the slaves were sold to men like Clow who brought them on board. Newton reluctantly did business with his old master and actually picked limes from the row of trees he had planted. Once on board, the men were herded below. Slaves were priced at so many « bars », and a bar would be made up of an assortment of those guns, pots and oddments in the vessel's hold. The grisly business of dealing in human flesh is well told in Newton's log: « Saturday, 29th December... At 2.a.m. the yawl came on board, brought six slaves, one woman, two boys, and three girls, all small. Numbers 38 to 43 ». « Wednesday, 20th March... Went on board the sloop, bought a cask of pork for Mr. Tucker, who came on board about noon with four slaves, two men, one woman girl, and one woman with a small child; settled accounts with him and paid him the balance ». « Wednesday, 8th May... Had George and Peter on board to dinner by invitation. Bought a man slave from the former, and a small boy from a canoe that came from the lowland, likewise a goat. » Slaves were traded in much the same way as a cask of pork or a goat.

SLAVES BELOW DECK

Life on board was dangerously unhealthy. No ship sailed without its colony of rats which chewed and soiled everything. John lamented the fact that much time was spent repairing the spare sails, which he could not mend half so fast as the rats destroyed them. He had so many on board that they were threatening to eat everything; they bit at the sailors and slaves when they caught them asleep and even nibbled at the cables.

At night the *Argyle's* hold was crammed with one hundred and seventy four slaves by the time she was ready to leave the coast. The sweating, steaming bodies lay packed together and disease and dysentery spread with alarming rapidity. Few weeks passed without one or more of the human cargo succumbing to the stench of the filthy air below decks. When a slave died Newton brought the rest on deck to air them; he ordered his crew to scrape the rooms, smoke the ship with tar, tobacco and brimstone for two hours and afterwards wash it with vinegar. As often as possible, weather permitting, the men were paraded on deck, washed down with brine and rinsed off with fresh water. But still they died and disease ravaged his crew also, carrying off his doctor, mate and carpenter. John informed Jack of the unpleasant but necessary duty when they slipped the black and white bodies into the shark infested waters where « these voracious animals... give such due attendance that the corpse had no sooner touched the water, than it is immediately torn to pieces, and devoured before our faces ».

The number of women on board and the absolute power of the captain presented a temptation that few masters had interest in resisting. But John was now of a different mind and he disciplined himself and, as far as their ship-board life was concerned, his crew also. He did not hesitate to put one of his sailors in irons for misusing a female slave, and throughout his voyages as captain John abstained from eating meat as a means, so he thought, of helping to control his

85

passions.   The contrast of this strange captain with
the life of those around him was not hard to discern.   He could see in them what he once was.   With
hearts eaten out by habitual sin and cruelty these men
were slaves to their passions and many of them knew
nothing of human tenderness.   When, in later years,
he campaigned against this awful trade, Newton could
recall the captain who, prevented from sleeping by the
crying of the baby of a woman slave, left his cabin,
walked below deck, snatched the child from the
mother's arms and threw it into the sea.   This horrifying spectacle was only surpassed by those who deliberately threw negroes overboard so that their loss
could be charged upon the insurer.

This strange captain put up with a good deal of
laughing abuse from the other captains.   They could
not understand a man who prayed, read his Bible and
wrote letters to his wife.   « They *think* I have not a
right notion of life », he wrote in one of those letters,
« and I *am sure* they have not.   They say I am melancholy; I tell them they are mad.   They say, I am a
slave to one woman, which I deny; but can prove that
some of them are mere slaves to a hundred.   They
wonder at my humour; I pity theirs.   They can form
no idea of my happiness. »   Of this fact John was
satisfied, for he confessed he would have been a-
shamed if such men, who « can be pleased with a
drunken debauch, or the smile of a prostitute »,
could understand his joy.   Apart from prayer, John's
only other escape from the distracting noise of slaves
and traders, the suffocating heat and the perpetual
talking, was to slip quietly onto the deck at night and
breathe out, « my dearest Mary », into the chill quiet-

ness of the starry sky.   He would never mention her name to others for to use it in the presence of « mere sailors » would be to degrade it.

At the close of a successful voyage John turned his ship home and ran before a healthy wind that carried him, at the rate of one hundred and eighty miles a day, into the company of Mary.   He arrived in Liverpool on Tuesday, October 8th, 1751, but was unable to reach Mary until November 2nd.

AN ADVENTURE IN READING

A sea-captain had little enough time to enjoy the comforts of his home and by April John had returned to Liverpool for the launching of a new ship which he was to command on his second voyage.   The *African*, another « Snow », he described as « one of the strongest vessels that can be built for money... but she is a very indifferent sailer ».

On Tuesday, 30th June the *African* unmoored and set out on her long voyage.   By August 13th, Newton was purchasing his first consignment of slaves, and a month later, in obedience to an Act of Parliament, the *African* adopted the new Gregorian Calendar which brought Newton's homeland, and his little ship, into line with the rest of Europe.   On this journey John had determined to be even more disciplined than before; accordingly he settled his life into a regular routine allowing time for devotion, study, exercise, and rest.   He would never sleep more than six or seven hours, began each day with an hour or two of Bible reading and then, as duty allowed, continued with his study of Latin, French and mathematics. Around mid-day he returned to prayer.

Apart from Euclid and Horace, John had read very little in his life, but the soul cannot grow by the study of geometry and Latin verse. During his brief time at home Newton had come across a book that caught his imagination for it seemed a mirror of his own life. It was *The Life of Colonel James Gardiner* and was written by Philip Doddridge. Doddridge, a dissenting minister in Northampton, friend of Isaac Watts and himself a hymn-writer of great ability, was personally acquainted with the Colonel who fell heroically on September 21st, 1745, in the ill-fated battle of Preston-Pans, a disastrous attempt to quell the army of the Young Pretender. Gardiner began his career in the army in such a wild and debonair fashion that he was referred to as « the happy rake » by all who knew him at the French Court, where he was employed in diplomatic affairs. It was whilst he was waiting for a midnight appointment with a married woman that he turned idly to a little book by Thomas Watson called *The Christian Soldier; or, Heaven taken by Storm*. Suddenly a light fell upon the page and Gardiner received such a visible representation of Christ upon the cross, surrounded by glory, that his life was changed; his illicit affairs were at once broken off and he became an unashamed Christian soldier. It was the self-discipline of Gardiner that set the pattern for Newton.

About this time also John began to read another

book by Doddridge, *The Rise and Progress of Religion in the Soul;* it was originally planned by Watts, but failing health cast the burden to his friend. This was a practical book that seemed to have been written for John Newton alone. His first glance at some of the chapter headings was sufficient to convince him of this: « The careless sinner awakened », « The reader reminded how much he needs the assistance of the Spirit of God », « The sad case of a relapse into known and deliberate sin, after solemn acts of dedication to God ». Doddridge spared neither diagnosis nor cure and John's soul leapt at the comfort offered. On the *Brownlow* he had yielded and his case had become deplorable but the wise doctor encouraged him that his « gangrene is not incurable... There is a balm in Gilead, there is a Physician there. Renew your application to Jesus that His blood may (as it were) be sprinkled upon you, that your soul may thereby be purified, and your guilt removed ». Such comfort slid into Newton's soul, bringing with it a joyful peace.

But not all was peace and perhaps it was the chapter entitled, « The established Christian urged to usefulness » that most goaded him at this time. He was urged to survey his life and see what opportunities of usefulness lay before him. « Has God invested you with power whether it be in a larger or smaller society? » wrote the hymn-writer of Northampton. « Remember that this power was given you that God might be honoured, and that those placed under your government, whether domestic or public, might be made happy. » Usefulness! John had never thought of that. On July 24th, 1751, he examined his life and wrote home to Mary: « I have now lived twenty-seven years, but how few things have I done really worthy of life ».   The right books were beginning to mould his thinking.

John set out to arrange his « Sea-Sunday » in a more useful way.   He described it to Mary during his third voyage in 1754.   He rose at four, commended the day and Mary to God, and took « a serious walk upon deck ».   This was followed by two or three chapters of Scripture, breakfast, and at eleven o'clock « the ship's bell rings my own little congregation about me ».   The captain read the morning service from the Book of Common Prayer, dismissed the crew and walked the deck until lunch.   In the afternoon he gathered his crew once more for service.   John did not hesitate to adapt the liturgy to suit the needs of his men.

John's concern for his crew is evidenced by the letter he wrote to Dr. Jennings, a dissenting minister at Wapping near London, with whom he frequently corresponded.   In this letter John urged that someone be found to write a book of counsel and devotions entirely suited to seamen; he promised to purchase one hundred at once and obtain orders for more if they would cost no more than two shillings a copy.   He similarly urged the reprinting of *Navigation Spiritualized* by John Flavel, a non-conformist minister at Dartmouth from 1656 to his death in 1691.

MUTINY

John had good reason to long for the improvement of his crew.   During the month of November, fever hit the boatswain and three sailors and thus seriously weakened the captain's manpower, particularly at a time when a number of the crew were away from the ship trading. To heighten his concern, Newton was informed by one of his sailors that one, Richard Swain, was soliciting members of the crew and planning a mutiny. This placed the captain in a most precarious position. With an increasing number of slaves on board, four members of his crew sick and half of the rest away in the yawl, Newton now could not even be certain who was for him and who was planning his death. When Swain arrived back in the yawl, the captain immediately placed him in irons, much to the apparent surprise of the sailor, who strongly protested his innocence. But still Newton did not know who was « in the gang ». Two days later an ordinary seaman reported to the captain that he had overheard a conversation between Swain and another crew member, during which they planned the death of the first mate and doctor, and an armed take-over of the ship. The identity of the mutineers was now revealed and Newton placed them in irons and later handed Swain and another member to the *Earl of Halifax* with the request that they be placed on board the first man-of-war encountered. Providentially, on the very day the plot was to have been executed, two of the chief parties were taken ill and one died within a week. John was saddened by this episode as he could discover no cause for such mutiny. He returned to his cabin and sat down to write to Mary; anxious not to worry her with such a chilling experience he excused his recent silence by offering a brief apology: « It has been out of my power to write of late. A part of the time I was on shore, and the rest indispensibly engaged » !

But it was soon the turn of the slaves. Some of the younger boys were allowed the freedom afforded to the women, and during the night of December 10th, shortly after the captain had concluded his Sunday service, dismissed the crew, and taken his last stroll around the deck, four negro boys slipped quietly to the grating covering the hold and dropped knives, a coal chisel and an assortment of tools to the men shackled below. While the captain and crew slept, the slaves worked. In the morning the captain made his rounds and discovered two men with their irons almost off. A search was ordered, the tools discovered and the slaves duly punished. Four of the ring leaders were fitted with iron collars and four boys were put « slightly in the thumbscrews to urge them to a full confession ». To be fair, Newton used this dreadful torture only twice throughout his commands; a remarkable restraint among slave captains. For the next few weeks the slaves were subdued but sulking and watching always for an opportunity to escape. This was not the first attempt of escape that Newton met with among his cargo. During his first voyage on the *Duke of Argyle* he discovered no fewer than twenty who had broken their irons with a large marline spike and were ready to attack when they were discovered, overpowered and resecured in the hold. On this coast there were many instances of whole crews murdered by escaping slaves.

This second journey was one of the most dangerous Newton ever undertook and by February 1753 he was trying to rid himself of a false charge laid against him by one of the half-caste traders. A strange foreboding prevented him leaving his ship as usual on a particular day and he later discovered that had he arrived on shore it would have been at the hazard of his life, for the trader had planned to expose an alleged crime and poison the captain.

MARY IS DEAD

It is hardly surprising that Newton, who years later wondered that so many English captains ever left the coast alive, was glad he could turn the *African* away from Sierra Leone and into the Middle Passage. But at the end of this journey another shock waited for him.

At the West Indian island of St. Christopher, more commonly known to the captains as St. Kitts, John looked eagerly for the anticipated packet of letters from his wife. But there was no post addressed to Captain Newton. His face blanched, his heart hammered, a searing knife seemed to cut into the pit of his stomach and John Newton sank into his chair. Mary was dead, she must be; there could be no other explanation. He enquired of every ship for letters, the captains came on board with their condolences and with a dogged routine he wrote a letter to his idol. « But to what purpose do I write » he penned in despair, « when perhaps my dear Mary may be past the power of reading? »

John lost his appetite, felt an incessant pain in his stomach and within three weeks considered himself under the weight of an awful stroke. He had never deserved Mary, that he knew, but he could not reconcile himself to the thought of losing her. As a last despairing gesture he sent off a boat to Antigua in case the letters had been misdirected. A packet of letters returned, six of them in the neat, familiar handwriting of Mary. « Oh how kind and careful is my dear », wrote John in ecstasy, and Newton, now the toast of all the captains, returned to his business of selling wives and husbands a continent apart.

In August 1753 the *African*, having disgorged two hundred and seven slaves, returned home with a cargo of cotton, sugar and rum after « a long, troublesome and precarious voyage », but with « entire satisfaction to myself, my friends and my employers ».

THE LAST VOYAGE

John Newton's final journey commenced on Sunday, 21st October when, in a light breeze, he weighed anchor and, with a crew of twenty-seven, took the *African* out to West Africa.

On this journey John took with him a young man named Job Lewis. He met him accidentally on the quayside at Liverpool and, when the owner of Lewis's ship went bankrupt, John offered to take him on board. Explaining his apparent care to Mary, Newton wrote simply: « There are other reasons for my concern, which I need not mention to you ». Those reasons could be found on board *H.M.S. Harwich* where Newton, newly converted to Shaftesbury's free thinking, perverted the mind of this impressionable young man to the same ugly trend. Lewis was now as careless as Newton had been, and with a sense of grief and conviction the older man hoped to lead Job to a better state. His intention was better than his judgement.

One month out of Liverpool Captain Newton apprehended an officer and a seaman for stealing. He put them in irons and the following day, the facts being proved, he « discharged them at the gangway »—the officer received 17 lashes and the seaman 11. But then, they had only been on board for a few « Sea-Sundays ». More could have been expected of the carpenter who in December 1753 gave trouble and received « two-dozen stripes ». It is fair to assume that these, and not the liturgy, sent him faithfully back to work two days later.

Job Lewis was the greatest trial to Newton. The young man's profanity and loose morality was a mirror of his own early life and at every turn and twist in Job's wretched life John felt an accusing finger pointing in his own direction. Any fool can sink a ship, but how hard it is to raise it from the bottom. Job scorned the « Sea-Sunday », laboured to undo the captain's influence on the crew and was generally a sharp thorn in Newton's side. At length, on the African coast, Newton purchased a small vessel, the *Racehorse,* fitted it for slaving, set up Lewis as captain and provided him with a crew. He went on board on January 18th and by the 21st of the following month was dead. He died of his excessively loose life and, according to those around him, left this world in rage and despair, « pronouncing his own fatal doom before he expired, without any appearance that he either hoped or asked for mercy ».

1754 was a terrible season for death on the African coast; John could not recall another like it, yet by April 8th he reported gratefully to his wife that he was in perfect health, and had buried neither white nor black. He wrote too soon. Shortly afterwards he was met by a fever that for three days raged so fiercely that both he and his crew despaired of his life. John confessed that he was ready to die but there was one excuse with which he covered his desire to live. It was the prompting of that chapter in Doddridge's *Rise and Progress of Religion;* he longed « that I might have opportunity of doing something for the glory of God, and the good of my fellow-creatures, that I might not go quite useless out of the world ». John felt he had so little used his present opportunities that he hardly dared to offer this plea. Nevertheless it was a prayer that God was to answer sooner than Newton anticipated.

The letters to his wife continued to pour out expressions of his love. « I find some new cause of endearment in you every day », he wrote in January. But they now contained much more than this. Shortly after his near-fatal fever, John wrote hopefully of his and Mary's faith in Christ. He was now sure that Mary shared with him a belief that nothing could enter their lives by chance and that they both depended wholly « on the divine mercy, through faith in the blood and mediation of Jesus Christ our Redeemer, according to the plain literal terms of the

Gospel ». Long pages spoke of his love for Christ and confidence in the truth. Mary could be in no doubt of her husband's deep commitment to the Saviour. As his ship sped homeward in July, Newton wrote triumphantly: « I need no-one to pronounce an absolution to me; I can tell myself that my sins are forgiven me, because I know in whom I have believed. This leads me to praise and adore him... »

If John learnt the value of Christian books on his second voyage, it was on this last journey that he learnt to appreciate Christian fellowship. Whilst anchored at Sandy Point, off the island of St. Christopher's, John met another Christian captain. It was a casual remark made at a gathering of captains that gave Newton a suspicion that this man knew something of Christ. He broached the subject carefully and the two men fell at once into close company. To Mary, John called him a valuable acquaintance, but withdrew the description that he was « of the same stamp » as Newton himself because, on reflection, « he is far beyond me in all that I most desire ». Alexander Clunie was a godly and experienced Christian. Each evening the two captains would meet in one or the other's cabin and by the pale and uncertain glow of the lantern they would read, pray and talk together. Clunie's example and conversation was of immense help. From this man John learnt his Christian doctrine. Clunie taught him the evangelical faith more carefully and warned him of those who deny the eternal deity of Christ and the historic truth of His Word. Until now John had thought every sermon must be good and every minister right. Alexander Clunie taught him to distinguish

97

things that differ. But he did more than this, he taught John to pray aloud and to witness more openly of his faith in Christ. The young Christian learnt the immense value of a wise teacher. It was from Clunie that John first learned that his salvation was by the initiative and sovereign power of God and in consequence it was a salvation that, once obtained, could never be lost. For two weeks Newton drank in the invigorating air of Christian fellowship and when he finally left for home he was in perfect peace, in spite of an unedifying ministry on this island where the clergyman's only distinguishing mark as a minister « was his gown and surplice ». John was learning to discern!

When the *African* returned to Liverpool in August, Joseph Manesty was well satisfied with his young captain. During the terrible Middle Passage he had lost neither slave nor sailor and this was highly commendable; he had well earned the flattering compliments that he received from every captain in port. Mary journeyed to Liverpool and remained with the Manestys whilst John fitted out a new and faster ship for another voyage. The *Bee* was ready to sail by November and John prepared to take that heart-rending farewell of his beloved Mary. The provisions were on board, the crew assembled, the barter stowed away and the captain was ready once more to pounce on the African coast, snatch parents and children from their native home and cast them into the cruel death of the plantations. Such were Newton's plans. But God ordered it otherwise.

CHAPTER 5.

CUSTOMS AND EXCISE

John and Mary sat in the parlour at the home of
Mr. and Mrs. Manesty. They were alone, drinking
tea together and talking over past events. The storm-
beaten face and spray-seared eyes of the captain gazed
at the youthful beauty of his wife. They talked. Any
conversation was satisfying so long as they could enjoy
just being together, before the mountainous seas and
howling winds tore them apart. Mary laughed at
John's clumsy proposal and he in turn reproached her
for the coldly proper replies his ardent letters had
received. They spoke of the sea, the sailors, and the
slaves. John expressed his dislike of a trade so perpet-
ually employed with chains, bolts and shackles and so
persistently separating him from Mary. But he knew
no other trade. At the age of thirty what else could
he do? He was a slave to slavery.

Suddenly the captain rose from his chair, lifted his
hand to his head and slumped to the floor. Mary
screamed, the Manestys and servants bundled into the
room, the doctor was hastily summoned and for an
hour John showed no signs of life other than breath-
ing. For her part, Mary fainted and sobbed alter-

nately and it took the best part of a year for her to recover from the shock. John was carried to his bed and, with dizziness and headaches, made his recovery.

The physicians suggested an apoplectic fit and there, although he had no recurrence throughout his life, the diagnosis rested. With such a condition it was unwise for Newton to return to the sea and within two days of sailing he resigned his command of the *Bee*. The man who took his place, most of the officers, and many of the crew, died at the hands of their slaves on that voyage and the vessel was brought home with great difficulty.

John took Mary to Chatham in the hope that away from the scene of his illness and in the familiar atmosphere of her home she would soon recover. But as he grew better, she declined and the physicians could neither diagnose nor remove her weakness. Mary became so frail that she could not bear anyone to walk across the room. For eleven months John watched anxiously and stood by that « dreadful post of observation, darker every hour ».

There was little possibility of work but the need was not urgent. He and Mary were welcome at the Catletts' home and although his monthly pay as a master had only been five pounds, he was allowed a share of the profits which, on the second voyage alone, amounted to two hundred and fifty seven pounds three shillings and eleven pence. With his immediate anxiety settled upon Mary, John set out to make the most of the time he spent in Kent.

THE RIGHT COMPANY

Alexander Clunie had had the foresight to recommend to Newton certain men who could help him grow in his faith, if ever he was close by London. Chatham was only a few hours' journey away and thus John frequently kissed his wife goodbye and visited the city. He listened to Clunie's pastor, the Rev. Samuel Brewer, a Congregational minister at Stepney. An introduction to the wise pastor greatly assisted John and for the first time he held spiritual counsel with a minister of God. He little knew that thirty years later men and women from all over the kingdom would call at his own home in the city of London to receive such counsel from his own lips. In London John was introduced to George Whitefield, a man of whom he had heard so much but of whom he felt he knew so little, to Christian societies, and many Christian friends. There was little to compare with this in Chatham and, but for Mary's failing health, he would have spent far more of his time in the city.

Mary became weaker and the fear of an earthly separation and the anxiety of future employment threw John into a turmoil of faith. He was unwilling to resign Mary and unable to return to the sea. Manesty promised to help all he could but the trade was over-worked and the merchant dared not venture another ship until the *Bee* returned. John paced the leafy lanes of Chatham and prayed in wooded fields bordering the Medway.

If John's money was wasting, his time certainly was not. He travelled often to London, sometimes by boat from Gravesend, walking the deck to avoid the foulness of the language below! He would rise at 4 a.m. to be at Whitefield's Tabernacle for the sermon and, after a service lasting three hours, « went away rejoicing » to hear Mr. Brewer! John had seen Moorfields as full of lanterns at 5 a.m. on a winter's morning « as the Haymarket is full of flambeaux (lighted torches) on an opera night ».

George Whitefield had passed his fortieth year and was shuttling between North America and England engaged in his powerful evangelistic work. An ordained clergyman of the Church of England and a graduate of Oxford, Whitefield (together with the Wesley brothers) had scandalized the polite and formal religion of his day by proclaiming the necessity of the new birth, and by daring to preach it in the open fields whenever a pulpit was denied him. His preaching offended, if only because it was true. In a reply to Lady Huntingdon, who had invited her to hear Whitefield preach, the Duchess of Buckingham well assessed his message when she complained: « It is monstrous to be told that you have a heart as sinful as the common wretches that crawl on the earth. This is highly offensive and insulting; and I cannot but wonder that your ladyship should relish any sentiments so much at variance with high rank and good breeding ». However her ladyship *did* believe such « monstrous » truth and the Duchess accepted the invitation! But multitudes knew Whitefield's message was true and upwards of thirty thousand people poured into the fields and commons to hear him preach. The evangelical revival was sweeping the country. John also knew the message was true, and he knew that Whitefield was right when he insisted that salvation was a work of God and that no man could become a Christian without the Holy Spirit first awakening his conscience and giving him faith to believe. John's own experience told him that, if nothing else. He became much drawn to these despised « Methodists » as Whitefield, the Wesleys and their followers were called.

In June 1755 Newton had visited Whitefield for just five minutes but the brief encounter developed into a lifelong friendship. John heard all the evangelical men in London: Mr. Romaine, who had newly settled at St. Anne's, and « Bold Bradbury », the rugged and fiery dissenter who had offended Queen Anne and was now in his sixtieth year of preaching. From these men, faithful to the teaching of the Scriptures, John Newton learned the breadth of the evangelical faith.

TIDE SURVEYOR

By August 1755 Joseph Manesty, true to his word, had procured for Newton the appointment of Tide Surveyor at Liverpool. John was reluctant to leave Mary who fared only worse at the hands of the physicians. In an age when the dozen or more cures for consumption consisted of such alternatives as « snayle-water » (a peck of garden snails roasted and mixed with chopped earth-worms and ale, herbs and numerous other ingredients!), or raw turnips and brown sugar candy, it is hardly surprising that John was not happy to leave his wife. Medicine was bursting with liberty, and pills, powders and potions were available for every ailment. Even electrotherapy had entered the field and doubtless Mary was « electrified »; after all, was not John Wesley tempted to refer to it a few years later as the « nearest to universal medicine of any yet known in the world »? John Newton was so impressed by this wonder that once installed at Liverpool, he invested in an electric machine and set up a private practice. He was still using it at Olney many years later and spoke of a poor rheumatic woman who came to him for treatment; it is doubtful whether the machine helped her, but Newton was able to record that whilst staying at Olney for treatment she listened to his sermons and came under conviction of sin! The physicians were gaining valuable experience in treating nervous disorders and with a king soon to be certified insane they were already applying blisters to heads to draw out poisons in the brain. With all the paraphernalia of eighteenth century medicine at her disposal the miracle was not that Mary recovered, but that she did not die!

The way in which Newton obtained his post of Tide Surveyor was quite remarkable. Manesty was under the impression that Newton's predecessor in the office was about to resign and, accordingly, he applied for the post on behalf of John. In fact the holder of the office had no intention of resigning but the day following the receipt of Newton's application the Tide Surveyor was found dead in his bed! As soon as this was known, the Mayor of Liverpool applied for the now vacant post for his nephew, but, by Manesty's strange mistake, Newton's application was already to hand. Nor was this all; a much inferior job had been first proposed to Newton and, but for Manesty's error, John would have accepted this employment.

John entered his new office as Tide Surveyor on August 19th, 1755. It was the heyday of smuggling and the Isle of Man, still duty free, was a valuable off-loading point for privateer vessels from America and the West Indies. To stem this illicit yet increasing trade, customs boats patrolled the waters, the Riding Officer combed the lonely beaches and cliffs, and the Tide Surveyor checked the vessels entering the harbour. As a Customs and Excise officer Newton's task was not always easy, but he entered upon it with a good heart. Sometimes his work was « a party of pleasure », but elsewhere he wrote of a « bustling tempestuous week ».

The city to which John Newton came in 1755 was growing rapidly in trade and influence. Early in the eighteenth century a building boom saw the erection of a new church, a charity school, the Bluecoat Hospital, an infirmary, a glass works, a salt works, sugar refineries, an iron foundry, copper works and many more industries. Over half a million pounds were spent in building projects during the first half of the century. Shipbuilding and repair yards grew up and the mercantile importance of Liverpool rivalled London and Bristol. The fine Georgian homes of the merchants were situated in Duke Street, Park Lane and Great George's Street, although many still preferred to live above their shops and offices in the narrow, dirty streets. The Excise Office, at this time of growing trade, privateering and piracy, was found in Paradise Street!

John described his situation to Mary. His duty was to visit the ships that arrived and check them for contraband; the following week he was required to inspect the vessels in the docks « and thus alternately the year round ». He was provided with a good office, a fire, a candle and between fifty and sixty people under his command. To transport the Tide Surveyor in style the Customs House supplied a handsome six-oared boat and a coxswain. John liked his station and declared to his wife: « I shall soon be

The custom house and the Old Dock with the spire of St. Thomas's church.

master of it ». He was! Within the first week he had seized contraband to the value of one hundred pounds two shillings and three pence, chiefly tobacco and coffee. Half this amount was awarded to Newton. However, such discoveries were not common, and during his nine years' service there are only twelve entries credited to Newton in *The Register of Seizures*.

On a bitter cold winter's night Newton would be rowed against strong tides and gales to meet an incoming vessel. He admitted that boarding a vessel in these conditions was not very agreeable. At other times he could be found in the early hours of the morning on watch at his office, warming himself by the fire and alternately writing to and praying for his beloved Mary. John longed for her to join him at Liverpool, but she was too frail to make such a long and arduous journey. With a salary of fifty pounds a year, a share of seizures which averaged sixty four pounds a year and many other incidentals to which a Tide Surveyor could legitimately lay claim, he could well afford to keep his wife in this city. But all John could do at present was to worry for her safety, whilst she in turn dutifully worried for his. September was a month of heavy storms and Mary lay in bed imagining her husband tossed and wrecked; she wrote of her nightly fears, only to be reassured by John that on the night of a particularly violent storm, to which she referred, he was safely in bed! He told her that a little practice would teach her not to worry for him. Meanwhile John went on worrying over Mary.

What John did not tell Mary was an experience that, but for the hand of God, would have certainly left her a young widow. After his conversion Newton was, throughout his life, a man remarkable for his punctuality. Those who worked under him could settle the hour of day by the arrival of the Tide Surveyor. One day he was a little detained in business and arrived at his boat a few minutes later than arranged to inspect a vessel lying out in the harbour. Newton went out in the boat and when he was a few minutes from reaching her, the ship blew up and sank killing all on board. But for that annoying and unexpected delay John would have been on board at the time of the explosion.

The letters to his wife were at this time full of rich encouragement. Mary, in her bodily weakness, had been tempted to doubt her personal salvation, but John urged her: « Go on, my dearest, I trust you are in the right way, wait patiently upon the Lord. Cast not away the confidence you express in his mercy, for in keeping it you will find a great reward. Greater is He that is with us, than he that is in the world. Changes you must expect. The Christian life is warfare; and though the captain of our salvation, by conquering for us, has secured us the final victory, we may be sorely pinched, and sometimes wounded while on the field of battle; but there is healing balm provided, and he will be always near to apply it ». Mary moved nearer London and there « picked up a fine set of methodistic-al acquaintances » which pleased John as immensely as it worried her aunt! Mary's spiritual life and assurance grew and by the tone of her letters John knew just where she stood. « Now my highest wishes are answered », he wrote on September 30th, « if my dearest Mary is partaker of the same hope with myself. How pleasant will all the future comforts and blessings which the Lord may be pleased to afford us prove, if we can discern them conveyed to us in the channel of redeeming love! » He noted with satisfac-tion that she had begun to take a stand for the truth; she too was listening to Mr Brewer and found that hearing of the great Physician had done her more good than all her medicines. Mary was no longer interested in cards, parties and the theatre; she sought the serious company of christians.

Yet true religion for the Newtons was nothing unsociable or gloomy; on the contrary, according to John it was the source of « peace, cheerfulness, and good humour ». John began to love Christian ministers and the people of the Lord and found their company a great delight, though he had to confess there were too few in Liverpool who cared for the things of God. The forty thousand inhabitants were more interested in the theatre and virtually went into mourning when the players left.

LUNCH WITH WHITEFIELD

When George Whitefield came to Liverpool early in September 1755 he could be sure of a welcome from Newton to make up for the coolness of the City Corporation; even the great preacher himself admitted he had been in few places with less encouragement. Within a week John had heard Whitefield preach nine times, and taken a meal with him on five occasions. The fire of the evangelist's zeal caught Newton also and one of his first attempts was to persuade his landlady to join him at one of the sermons. She attended very diffidently, (in fact her first response to the invitation had been plainly rude) but was so interested that she asked her tenant for a copy of Whitefield's printed sermons and went a second time. To his great joy this lady suggested they might ask the eminent gentleman to lunch one Sunday. John needed no further encouragement. He immediately determined to contribute to the extra cost of the meal and improved the occasion by inviting four or five Christian friends to join the party!

On September 14th John accompanied Whitefield to the morning service at St. Thomas's Church; there they listened to a man the very opposite of the great evangelist. « No life in his delivery, no gospel in his discourse », John commented. However, this was the day for George Whitefield to come home to lunch with Newton, his landlady and those few select friends. In the afternoon Whitefield took his stand in St. Thomas's Square and at five o'clock was preaching to almost four thousand people.

George and John became close friends. The one talked and the other listened. John had so much to learn and, though he was reading and studying as often as his duties allowed (he began with Greek, commenced Hebrew a year later and two years after that was working at Syriac), there was so much that could only be grasped in conversation. Whitefield was clear and concise. He believed firmly in the old Calvinistic doctrines: that personal salvation was by the sovereign choice of God and that those who were chosen to eternal life were given the Holy Spirit who alone enabled them to believe the Gospel. John had always known this from the experience of his own helpless condition before God opened his mind in that Atlantic storm, but now Whitefield turned him to the Scriptures to find it in the warp and woof of the Word of God. George also showed John the glorious hope

110

Whitefield took his stand in St. Thomas's Square.

of eternal salvation and explained from Scripture the impossibility of losing a salvation once applied by Christ. Even John Wesley cavilled at this doctrine, but Newton had learned sufficient of his own heart by his backsliding on the *Brownlow* to know that unless God kept him « in Christ », there could be no hope for him. Whitefield also believed in hell. Dr Johnson once declared: « I am afraid I may be one of those who shall be damned », and when asked what he meant by this he replied passionately and loudly: « Sent to Hell, Sir, and punished everlastingly ». That was not popular, and never has been, but the Bible taught it so Whitefield preached it and John Newton, knowing he had deserved it, believed it.

Some of his acquaintances referred to Newton as « Young Whitefield », but the sea captain, who had been ridiculed in Africa and the West Indies for his strange views, was hardly likely to take this ragging as anything other than a high compliment.

The visit of Whitefield not only taught John's mind, but it fired his heart, and soon after that first evangelistic effort for his landlady, John found himself engaged in his first pastoral visit. It was to the home of a man who had lost his wife in child-bearing in the first year of their marriage. Such visits would later become common-place in the life of a minister in those days of appallingly high mortality in child-birth. John did his best to comfort, yet felt so unable to help. « It is only God who can give comfort in such a case », he wrote to Mary; and in a very real sense he could never hope to become more professional than that.

MARY IN LIVERPOOL

By October, Mary was sufficiently recovered to make that tedious journey to Liverpool. It was hardly the best month for travel, but if she had not set out then the roads would have turned into their usual winter quagmire and the journey would be impossible. Four years later John tried this route in January and the road from Everton to York was so bad that he feared for his poor horse and expressed his concern to Mary: « Lest I must have left him sticking in the clay, as a memorandum of my having passed that way ». In one day he covered barely eighteen miles, and six of those were out of his way on a wrong road. Admittedly John had a mount that was rather slow and refused to mend his pace to please anybody, but even allowing for this the rider met a ten mile stretch between York and Leicester that was so bad he declared his willingness to detour a hundred miles rather than traverse that part again. In the winter, coaches stuck fast in the mud; even the highwayman could only plod to his scene of banditry and thousands of villages were marooned until the spring.

But Mary arrived, tired and weak, yet in one piece and delighted to be with her husband once more. Although Mary returned to London on occasions, the Newtons were together for most of their remaining time in Liverpool.

1756 was the year in which Britain commenced her « Seven Years' War » with France; the fever of war paralysed the nation in those early months and Liverpool lost two out of every five ships that sailed from

113

her port.   Conscripts were hustled into the barracks, and the press-gangs once more roamed the coast and countryside.   In the relative peace and calm of the Newtons' home, John began reading prayers to the family.   From time to time he would comment upon the passage he read, but it did not come easily and he felt not a little embarrassed in the presence of a few friends, a servant and Mary.   But he persisted.

They were busy and happy years at Liverpool and after the long separations from Mary it was a joy for them to be together again.   Mary, although frail, regained much of her strength and they threw themselves into what little, real, spiritual life existed in the city.   John complained sadly of the many ministers who « slighted and degraded » Jesus by their false doctrines, but he found fellowship with Mr Oulton and his Baptist meeting (though never able to accept their insistence upon the immersion of adults only) and a little fellowship with the Wesleyan Methodists; but this last group was narrow and bigoted and Newton urged John Wesley to bring them to a more warm and friendly frame of mind.   Already, John and Mary found themselves placing less emphasis upon a denominational stand and more upon the vital truths of evangelical Christianity.

TOWARDS THE MINISTRY

John had not yet preached a sermon, but he had published one or two short articles that were well received.   Newton's mother had longed and prayed that her son might enter the ministry and when he reflected upon Paul's words in Gal. 1: 23,24 his mind turned in that direction. He read: « But they had heard only, that he which persecuted us in times past now preached the faith which once he destroy- ed. And they glorified God in me ». That, John longed to do also. If any man had a message, John Newton had, yet his first attempt at preaching was little short of disastrous.

There was little evangelical preaching in Liverpool and John and Mary took the opportunity to visit Yorkshire and see for themselves the work of the Spirit in the area of which they had heard so much. They arrived at Leeds one day in 1758 and John was invited to preach at White Chapel for the minister, the Rev. Mr Edwards. Newton prepared his sermon carefully, but determined, in true Methodist style, to take no notes into the pulpit. After tea Mr Edwards invited Newton to leave the company and spend a short while alone if he wished; John declined affirming that he was well prepared. The service began and the congregation waited eagerly to hear the sermon from a man with such a testimony. John read out his text: « I have set the Lord always before me, because he is at my right hand, I shall not be moved ». He began fluently but after a few minutes his behaviour belied the truth of his text. As if blown by a gust of wind, John's outline fled from his mind; he stumbled, paus- ed, rallied, only to fall again and finally, utterly confused, urged the pastor to conclude the sermon for him. Mr Edwards took up the theme as poor John Newton hung his head and left the pulpit in shame. For a while, he felt so keenly his failure that, whenever he met two or three people talking in the street, John was convinced they were speaking of his disastrous entry into preaching. But it was a valuable lesson and one he never forgot. Although John Newton did not often preach with notes he never again tried to preach without the aid of the Holy Spirit. His next attempt at preaching met with little more success even though he guaranteed that he and his congregation would endure to the end. John wrote out his sermon in full and read it like some dry lecture and, fearing that he might lose his place, he did not lift his eyes from the page once, until the journey was through! Years later when called upon to advise young men entering the ministry, Newton reminded them that to preach well nineteen times is no security for the twentieth and, even after being upheld for twenty years, if the Lord should remove his hand, the preacher would be as much at a loss as he was at the first.

However, encouraged by some friends, but not yet knowing whether he could ever stand in public and preach regularly, he applied to the Bishop of Chester in December 1758. The Bishop received him civilly and referred him to the Archbishop's chaplain, who passed him to the secretary, who refused him with « the softest refusal imaginable ». John Newton had not been to university and, worse still, he had Methodist acquaintances. When John Wesley visited Liverpool and learnt of Newton's refusal, he was angry at the authorities for snubbing such a valuable servant when, every day, idle and ignorant men were entering the church on the strength of a degree alone. Wesley urged Newton to become an itinerant preacher, like himself.

Undeterred, John began to write sermons which, unable to preach, he published. On January 1st, 1760, the year George III came to the throne, John's first sermons appeared under the title, *Six Discourses as Intended for the Pulpit.* He was not so tedious as to keep referring to his own life, but under such texts as « The heart is deceitful above all things and desperately wicked » (Jeremiah 17: 9,10) and « This is a faithful saying, and worthy of all acceptation that Jesus Christ came into the world to save sinners, of whom I am chief » (1 Timothy 1: 15), who else had he in mind? They were strong sermons, full of Scripture and doctrine, yet not long or heavy. John knew how to reach the heart.

Faced with the disinterest of the established church, John was tempted to become an itinerant preacher or even join the dissenters, for whom he held a high regard, but Mary, his « judicious and affectionate counsellor », saw to it that he kept to a straight course. He must wait for the Lord's time. He did wait, though impatiently, and John and Mary made a few more journeys into Yorkshire to see for themselves the progress of the evangelical Methodist revival.

How nearly John entered the dissenting ministry is seen in the fact that, early in 1764, he took up a three month appointment at a congregational chapel in Warwick. He was still Tide Surveyor but the war had not only hampered legitimate shipping, it largely curtailed smuggling also and Newton could be absent for long periods. John was not happy with the result of his preaching at Warwick and though he entered the town with God's promise to Paul, « Fear not, Paul, I have much people in this city », he soon learnt that Paul was not John, and that Corinth was not Warwick.   However, the congregation warmly urged him to stay and John gave the invitation serious consideration, much to the heated annoyance of Mary's brother Jack, who had already accused him of spending more of his concern upon his religious friends than upon his relatives.   Jack should have known better, for John was regularly pleading for his brother-in-law's salvation.   Sadly, by December 1764 Jack was dead.

In the following years John considered opening a meeting house in Liverpool from which he could preach, but it was wise Mary who vetoed that idea.   Instead, he wrote a survey of his life for the benefit of a young clergyman friend in Oxford. Thomas Haweis was so impressed that he asked John to expand the narrative.   He then sent it to a nobleman with whom he was acquainted and whom he knew to be a patron of the evangelicals.

A LETTER FROM DARTMOUTH

Early in 1764 John received an invitation from a Presbyterian church in Yorkshire, and his refusal for ordination by two archbishops and a bishop led him to feel that this was the door opening into the ministry.   Within a few days, however, another letter arrived which changed his mind and the course of his life.   The second letter came from Lord Dartmouth, the nobleman who had read those fourteen letters of Newton's life.   The Earl was offering him the curacy

118

of the parish church of St. Peter and St. Paul in the remote Buckinghamshire town of Olney. « Had the proposal been deferred one week », wrote Newton, « it would have been too late ».

William Legge, the second Earl of Dartmouth, was born in 1731, educated at Westminster School and Oxford and took his seat in the House of Lords on May 31st, 1754. The evangelical convictions of the Earl were apparent to all and it was these convictions that denied him a post of intimacy in the court of George III, « lest so sanctimonious a man should gain too far on His Majesty's piety ». It would have saved His Majesty a deal of suffering and unhappiness if he had! In addition to his appointment to the Privy Council in 1765, Lord Dartmouth served as President of the Board of Trade, Secretary of State for the Colonies and High Steward of Oxford University. He was not a great politician and spoke rarely in the House of Lords, but his sincerity and Christian faith marked him out. The poet Cowper referred to him as « one who wears a coronet and prays », in days when those two privileges were rarely combined in the same person. Dartmouth championed the cause of evangelicalism and for his association with the « enthusiastic » Methodists was nicknamed « The Psalm Singer ».

Newton met Dartmouth who introduced him to many influential friends including John Thornton. Thornton was reputed to be one of the wealthiest merchants in the country; he had entered the Russian trade with one hundred thousand pounds and by the time he died in 1790 his generosity was legendary among the evangelicals. He is reputed to have

119

given away more than one hundred and fifty thousand pounds. Newton had little conception of the future importance of this meeting.

April saw John once more in London to gain an interview with the Bishop of Chester. The beginning of his interview with the bishop was not encouraging. John suspected by his Lordship's behaviour that someone had written disparagingly of him from Liverpool. The bishop was about to examine the applicant more closely when Newton produced a letter from Dartmouth which he had received in London, one calculated to change the mind of any dignitary. Suddenly « a full stop was put to all enquiries, but what were agreeable »; the bishop became sociable, kept John in « chit-chat » for nearly an hour, wished him much success and passed him to the Bishop of Lincoln. This bishop examined Newton for an hour and John, so that he could never be charged with dishonesty, informed the prelate of the areas of doctrine in which he differed from the customary teaching of the respectable pulpits. But Lincoln was not offended, « declared himself satisfied » and within three weeks, on April 29th, 1764, ordained John Newton into deacons' orders of the Church of England. Within two months he was ordained a priest. On his return home, John detoured to Olney « just to take a glance at the place and the people ».

CHAPTER 6

THE COUNTRY CURATE

The Rev. John Newton leant against the old, gnarled elm at the northern end of the town and rested from his long journey.   Newport Pagnell lay six miles to the south, Bedford a little more to the east and Northampton almost twenty miles north-west.   The town itself lay at right angles to the River Ouse and the countryside around was flat and uninteresting.   What was more, the sea captain could reflect, he could hardly have found a parish further inland if he had tried!

If John's eye could have run the full length of the high street and over the old stone bridge at the far end, a plain picture would have presented itself to him.   Olney had little attraction in its eighteenth century appearance.   The main street was lined with uneven rows of mud-plastered cottages, whose bow windows and drooping thatched roofs gave the appearance of a straggling line of raw recruits before being drilled into formation.   The barber, William Wilson, advertised his shop with the customary striped pole and *The Swann,* one of the two inns of the town and, according to William Cowper, excessively careless

121

with the post, boasted a large, hideous, overhanging, wooden balcony. The high street of this out of the way town, which years later could still only boast « one barber, one bellman, and one poet », spilled into the triangular market place which was dominated by three large and stately elms. The poor houses respectfully withdrew from encroaching into this triangle

The high street spilled into the market place.

of trade, but clustered, as if for protection and warmth, around the Baptist meeting place and the large prison-like building of Orchard Side with its red bricks, flat roof and imitation battlements. The Independent, or Congregational chapel, erected in 1700 was nudged behind the houses off the main street and approached through a gateway just wide enough to admit a carriage. The market place itself displayed the Shiel Hall, an old two-storey stone building with a row of outside steps reaching to the upper storey, which served as both town hall and, after 1775, as Samuel Teedon's school-room; and a curious six-sided *Round House* that served as the town prison and stood in the centre of the market place as a lone sentinel to enforce the law. From here to the Independent chapel and back was the « whipping-distance » of Olney. A few more cottages and the blacksmith's forge completed the scene.

Although John Newton could not see all this as he leant against the elm trunk, his eye involuntarily picked up the spire of the parish church half a mile distant and followed its slim and graceful line into the sky. The present building was erected in the four-teenth century, though there was a church in Olney long before that. It was planted on the north bank of the Ouse at the extreme boundary of the town as if to protect the two thousand inhabitants of Olney from the violent winds that whipped across the open fields. The high street passed the church-yard and wandered onto the long stone bridge that straddled the river. Beyond the slow winding Ouse with its banks lined with stately elms, the new curate-in-charge gazed at the peaceful meadows sloping up to the horizon; grazing cattle and a solitary herdsman's hut filled out the scene.

Apart from the scattered farmsteads, the town was compact if not neat. The main street was surprisingly well constructed with a pitch or camber to drain it. It needed to be well laid; at least two main streams made their acquaintance just opposite the Independent chapel and for companionship travelled together into the river. At flood time they could take rather longer than usual to reach their destination. To the east of the church stood the Great House, a large old mansion owned by Lord Dartmouth, and farther still to the east stood Olney Mill.

In May, Newton moved his belongings into the old parsonage opposite the church-yard and sat down to write to Mary: « I am well, and as comfortably settled as I can desire during your absence ». Mary was again unwell, residing at Chatham and she did not reach Olney until the end of the summer.

« THE HALF-STARVED AND RAGGED »

John Newton, with the growing friendship of the Earl and the rich merchant, had moved into one of the poorest towns in the country. There were only two trades pursued in this place and most of the families followed both lace making and farming. The men eked out a pitiful existence on the land whilst the women supplemented the income by working ten hours a day at their lace pillows for the magnificent wage of four shillings a week, from which they deducted sixpence for their thread. The new curate was no stranger to poverty and he moved easily in and out of the cold stone cottages of this « half starved and ragged » people, as Cowper later described them.

Lace making was introduced into England around the year 1626 by Flemish refugees. By the early eighteenth century it was well established at Olney. The girls learnt the trade early, starting at five or six years of age in the Dames' Schools. Orchard Side was once a Dame's School and here the children worked for ten hours a day, paying sixpence a week to learn; this figure was reduced as they mastered the trade. When John entered one of the poor cottages

Working ten hours a day at their lace pillow.

on a winter's afternoon, he would find no fire in the iron grate, for the soot and smoke would spoil the lace; a « dicky-pot » helped to keep warm the feet of the women huddled round the single candle-stool. With the aid of the ingenious candle-stool, the light of one candle, diffused through glass flasks filled with water, would be sufficient to enable as many as eighteen

125

women to work at the expense of one penny each evening. Normally three or four women worked at the lace whilst another spun the yarn close-by. Each woman was bent over a large pillow, resting partly on her lap and partly on a stool. This was her lace-pillow on which she worked the intricate patterns of the exquisite lace so fashionable in the extravagant London society. Her pins were marshalled and moved like militia in a Lilliputian army, and her bobbins, worked with such speed that John could hardly keep his eye on the objects, were themselves things of art. No two bobbins were alike, though hundreds were used, and with names like « Dear Father », « Joey », « Ellen », each one told its own story and brought interest and conversation into a dull routine. There could be no mistaking the lace-maker's cottage; as he walked down the high street John was fascinated to stop at a door and listen to the women chanting their rhythmical verse to aid the movement of pins and bobbins:

> « Get to the field by one
> Gather the rod by two
> Tie it up by three
> Send it down home by four
> Make her work hard at five
> Give her her supper at six
> Send her to bed at seven
> Cover her up at eight... »

And so it continued. These « Lace Tells », as Newton came to know them, told stories, passed on gossip, moralised or simply revealed the hard, unending toil and dreary life of the lace maker. A stool, a bed, a table and a few pots were all these homes possessed.

William Cowper, who followed Newton past these doors a few years later, picked out the life of the lace-maker in his descriptive poem « Truth ».

> « Yon cottager who weaves at her own door,
> Pillow and bobbins all her little store,
> Content, though mean, and cheerful, if not gay,
> Shuffling her threads about the live-long day,
> Just earns a scanty pittance, and at night
> Lies down secure, her heart and pocket light... »

But this was not all, through the sound and careful instruction of their clergyman many of these poor women came to a knowledge of a truth, to which the great French philosopher and atheist, Voltaire, was stranger. Though she had little understanding yet she:

> « Just knows, and knows no more, her Bible true,
> A truth the brilliant Frenchman never knew,
> And in that charter reads with sparkling eyes,
> Her title to a treasure in the skies. »

PASTORAL CARE

Hunger was always just outside the door, and illness frequently intruded. John and Mary took this poor community close to their hearts and Newton found many in his congregation to be a « praying people » who, when Mary was away from home nursing her ailing father in 1775, prayed constantly for her and urged Newton to recall her.   He wrote simply: « You are greatly wanted by the sick, by the poor, and by your family ».

The eighteenth century was the century of absentee clergy and when Newton became curate-in-charge at Olney he had first to come to an arrangement with the old evangelical vicar Moses Browne who, having twelve children to care for, insisted upon twenty pounds a year from the modest fifty allowed to the incumbent.   Thirty pounds was barely sufficient for his needs, but neither John nor Mary was daunted.   The small investment Newton had with Manesty was entirely lost when the merchant went bankrupt two years after John settled in his new charge.   But John had received such disappointments before, and during his third voyage twelve years earlier he express-ed his thoughts to Mary: « This failure in dirty money matters is the only abatement we have hitherto met with... in other respects we have the advantage of those who are envied by the world... we want for nothing at present... perhaps we may not be rich—no mat-ter.   We are rich in love.   We are rich indeed if the promises and providence of God are our inherit-ance ».   Though John Newton later published his letters and sermons, which were very popular, and though he could claim the friendship of living for-tunes, yet John was never a wealthy man and the sums he received he promptly expended to the poor. John's call to Olney was clear and firm.   Shortly after he had settled in his new parish, some kind friends, mindful of his welfare, suggested that he should consider the offer of a large and affluent church at Hampstead; here the air was healthy, and the church was close to London, his friends and fellow ministers. To this tempting suggestion John could only conclude that: « the Lord knew that there would be vacancies elsewhere, before he led me to Olney ». And so he stayed.

It was this unworldly heart and pastoral care that took him into the homes of rich and poor alike. John's first sermon at Olney, preached on Sunday, May 27th, 1764 was based upon Psalm 80:1, « Give ear, O Shepherd of Israel, Thou that leadest Joseph like a flock »; for the next sixteen years he applied that sermon. The death of the thirteen year old son of a farm labourer cut John as if it were his own bereavement. The young lad, just home from school, had climbed upon the hay cart when another son drove off; the horse suddenly took fright, over-turned the cart and the poor boy fell under the wheel and was killed instantly. The pastor, for whom death was once a commonplace, necessary, part of his trade, visited the home to comfort the sobbing father and hysterical mother. They received him kindly and, with true understanding, he said very little at the grave side, « as the hour was late, and the parents brokenhearted ». The bereaved mother had long attended the Independent chapel but now came more regularly to the parish church!

John knew his people well. He frequently visited the poor cottage of Molly Mole, « the Mole Hill » he called it, where prayer was always offered; and when Molly moved home, the prayer meetings followed her. Whenever John was away, he would write home and send greetings to various villagers, listing them

129

carefully by name, and in the great houses he would mention the servants also. Typical of the pastor's care was a letter written to William Cowper whilst Newton was away in London: « I hope Molly Coles is recovering apace, and that the quarantine between the two houses will soon be taken off. Please to give my love to her, as likewise to Molly Mole (who I hope will be a very good girl), and to all the Marys, Mollys, Sallys, Sarahs etc. that come in your way—particularly Sally Johnson and Judith ».

There were few events in the town that evaded the scrutiny or care of the ever-watchful shepherd. When Mary was away from home he kept her informed of all the news: of the recent deaths and illnesses; of that broken engagement or sottish husband; of the good lady who fell into the river and nearly drowned and who, whilst recuperating, fell from a horse and was almost killed; of the girl who ran away with a soldier. But it was not gossip or scandal. These people mattered to John, and John and Mary mattered to them. In November 1775, when Mary was at Chatham, John wrote to her: « I told the people, on Sunday evening, my good news, and read your father's letter. Both he and you were earnestly prayed for ». But it was a season of great illness and scarcely a house in the town was at full strength. « I suppose more than a hundred were detained from us by colds and illness. »

John Newton was a welcome visitor in the homes or beside the men in the fields. Bobbins and plough were laid aside for a brief talk, possibly a hymn, and a prayer. Where John found a family eager to read a

Bible, but too poor to buy one, he could always find one for them. When a great snow fall in 1776 virtually marooned the town for some weeks, Newton hurriedly made collections for the relief of the poor.

Here was no country parson, riding and hunting with the squire or shut up in his vicarage stuffing his brain with philosophy and poetry; John Newton was disciplined in study, spending his mornings at his books and the Bible in preparation for his sermons, but much of his day was spent visiting the cottages or riding to some outlying farmstead, « in the concern of immortal souls, with eternity in view ».   The people at Olney quickly learned that John Newton's life as a parish minister was consistent with his pulpit ministry.   He himself once admirably linked the two when commenting to a friend: « I measure ministers by square measure.   I have no idea of the size of a table, if you only tell me how *long* it is; but if you also say how *wide*, I can tell its dimensions.   So when you tell me what a man is in the pulpit, you must also tell me what he is out of it, or I shall not know his size ».

THE PULPIT AND PEW

In July 1758 the pulpit at Olney had resounded to the eloquent and powerful voice of George Whitefield and the people were no strangers to evangelical doctrine.

John Newton was no great preacher and some thought he appeared to his least advantage in the pulpit.   Richard Cecil, his personal friend and biographer who admired Newton immensely, claimed that « his utterance was far from clear, and his attitudes ungraceful ».   His form and delivery of a sermon left much to be desired.   But the value of sermons is not to be assessed in that way.   John once confessed to a divinity student: « The Lord has sent me here, not to acquire the character of a ready speaker, but to win souls to Christ ».

John once complained of long sermons (he meant two hours) and believed it was better to feed the people like chickens, a little and often, than to cram them like turkeys till they cannot hold one gobbet more.   « Besides », he continued with a devastatingly practical concern, « over-long sermons break in upon family concerns, and often call off the thoughts from the sermon to the pudding at home, which is in danger of being over-boiled ».   He only spoke for an hour when he had little to say.   Contrary to the habit of the eighteenth century anglican, of reading sermons, Newton preferred extempore preaching, which gave him more freedom to appeal to the heart; he prepared his sermon, writing out his notes in a small hardback notebook, but entered his pulpit without it.   That first disastrous attempt at reading a sermon was a painful memory.

After preaching his first six sermons at Olney, John felt he had run through his whole stock.   He wandered out of the church-yard and down to the Ouse; there he watched the river on its long journey to the sea.   « How long has this river run? »   he thought. « Many hundreds of years, and so it will continue ».

132

He concluded: « Is not the fund for my sermons equally inexhaustible—the Word of God? ». Newton was never again afraid of running out.

John Newton spoke to the heart, kept his sermons within a reasonable time, and illustrated them in a lively way. Yet Newton saw to it that he never compromised his doctrine. So concerned was he to meet the needs of his entire congregation that he once preached from 2 Peter 1:10, « Chiefly on account of my maid Molly, who is perplexed and tempted on the point of election ». On another occasion he chose Hebrews 2:18 as his text because the poet Cowper was depressed in spirit, though he reported, « I do not think he was much the better for it, but perhaps it might suit others ».

Whatever limitations John had in the pulpit, the pews at Olney steadily filled and in July 1765 a large gallery was added to the north wall; but even when some of the congregation moved upstairs, others came in until there seemed no more room in the body of the church than before. The uncertain weather and dirty roads made little impression on his congregation and within his first year John could thankfully claim not only that the congregation was « large and serious » but also that rarely did a week pass without his learning of some person challenged or awakened.

In addition to the regular Sunday morning and afternoon services, John had a little company who came to his house on Sunday evening after tea, where they spent an hour in prayer and singing. The « little company » increased to over seventy and John was forced to limit the numbers and keep out those who only came to stare. By the end of his ministry in Olney that little company became an evening service and he expounded the First Epistle of Peter to them from 1776 to 1779. He established three special meetings, one for children, another for « young and enquiring persons » and a third for older Christians for prayer and Bible study. Newton also divided his people into small groups of eight to twelve members so that he could meet with them once every six weeks for conversation and prayer.

The Tuesday prayer meeting was soon attended by upwards of forty adults, and Newton, writing to his old friend Captain Clunie, just a year before the death of that excellent captain in 1770, informed him that they were soon to move to the Great Room in the Great House where they could accommodate upwards of one hundred and thirty people. To celebrate this removal in 1769, William Cowper composed the lovely hymn :

> « Jesus where'er Thy people meet,
> There they behold Thy mercy seat,
> Where'er they seek Thee, Thou art found,
> And every place is hallowed ground. »

The townspeople were prepared to walk through driving rain and freezing snow to attend the prayer meeting and Newton recorded gratefully that many of the younger and « lively sort » had commenced a 6 a.m. meeting for prayer on Sunday morning. William Cowper regularly attended and described it vividly: « On Sabbath mornings in winter I rose before

134

day and by the light of a Lanthorn trudged with Mrs Unwin, often through snow and rain to a prayer meeting at the Great House... There I always found forty or fifty poor folks who preferred a glimpse of the light of God's countenance and favour to the comforts of a warm bed, or to any comforts that the world could afford them and there I have often myself partaken that blessing with them ». These prayer meetings were the strength of Newton's ministry at Olney.

JOHN'S HOME AND STUDY

The old parsonage was very inconvenient for the wide ministry of John and Mary Newton and in 1767 Lord Dartmouth enlarged and practically rebuilt it so that John considered it « one of the best and most commodious houses in this county ». The house has remained virtually unchanged since then.

The publication of Newton's autobiography was one of the first events of his settlement at Olney. Under its original title: *An Authentic Narrative of Some Remarkable and Interesting Particulars in the Life of... communicated, in a series of Letters to the Rev. T.Haweis*, the book was, according to fashion, anonymous; however the name was soon inserted as Newton became well known. Those fourteen chapters startled many of the inhabitants and John found himself the object of their inquisitiveness. « The people stare at me since reading them, and well they may. I am indeed a wonder to many, a wonder to myself, especially I wonder that I wonder no more. » He believed

God had sent him to Olney so that if he achieved nothing more, people would see him walking down the street and recognise in his life the remarkable grace of God.

Visitors travelled for miles to see the man behind the *Authentic Narrative* and the vicarage was besieged with

One of the best houses in this county.

callers. It became a great inconvenience as it broke into John's pastoral duties and endangered his spirit by the many favours and distinctions offered him. Ministers of all persuasions came to the town where they heard « famous things » were happening; young students visited and stayed to sit under Newton's ministry; politicians arrived, and even an admiral came to talk with the man once beaten at the gangway for deserting his ship.

Unwittingly those hordes of visitors placed a great strain upon the slender budget of the Newton home. Mary managed efficiently and without complaining and there was little that poor John could do if she had. It was, therefore, with a deep sense of thankfulness to God that John and Mary opened a letter from John Thornton in which he urged them to be hospitable, to keep open home for those who were worthy of entertainment and to help the poor and needy. To back his request, the wealthy merchant promised Newton two hundred pounds a year, and more when it was required.

Their hospitality stretched wider and each Sunday John invited to lunch all who had walked more than six miles to church. But however full the house, it was empty without Mary. He wrote to her during her absence: « The house looks unfurnished without you, and I am missing you in every room ». He described himself moping around feeling thoroughly miserable. Mary, like any good wife, was the home. Towards the end of 1775 Mary brought her ailing father to the vicarage where he died just over a year later.

While Mary and the maid entertained with quiet dignity, John talked amiably until he could reasonably escape to the seclusion of his study. Here, at the top of the house in his little gabled room, John spread out his books or knelt to pray for Molly Mole and her cheerful witness, or for Sally Perry for whom there was little hope of recovery from her present illness, or for the ploughman who ill-treated his wife and starved his family, or for the many friends that the curate was meeting from far afield.

Above the fireplace in his study, John Newton painted two texts on the bare plaster; they read as a mirror of his life:

> « Since thou wast precious in my sight, thou hast been honourable.»
>
> (Isa. 43:4)

> « But thou shalt remember that thou wast a bondman in the land of Egypt,
> And the Lord thy God redeemed thee. »
>
> (Deut. 15:15)

There were two windows in this room. If Newton looked south he could see nothing but the churchyard, his church and the river and fields stretching away beyond it. But perhaps he placed his desk at the north window from which he could view a cluster of cottages around Orchard Side in one small corner of his town. It was in this room that John wrote his many hymns for the prayer meetings in the Great House and those long and profitable letters that were later published under the titles: *Omicron* and *Cardiphonia*. It was here also that Newton began his work *An Ecclesiastical History;* this was intended to be a history of the Christian Church but he did not progress beyond the first century! However the quality of his work was commended by the outstanding eighteenth century church historian, Joseph Milner, who, in the introduction to his own *History of the Church of Christ,* not only praised its excellence but claimed it

138

was the inspiration for his own work and that he originally contemplated beginning where Newton left off. Cowper thought Newton's style even better than Gibbon! In an age of great scholarship, Newton, with only two years of formal and very inferior education behind him, had well deserved such high praise. Shortly after he left Olney in 1780 John wrote with serious humour to his successor, Thomas Scott, « Methinks I see you sitting in my old corner in the study. I will warn you of one thing, that room (do not start) used to be haunted. I cannot say I ever saw or heard anything with my bodily organs, but I have been sure there were evil spirits in it and very near me—a spirit of folly, a spirit of indolence, a spirit of unbelief, and many others—indeed their name is legion. But why should I say they are in your study when they followed me to London, and still pester me here? »

« THEIR OWN LITTLE WAY »

John and Mary never had a family of their own. Early in 1753, on his second voyage as a sea captain, John commented upon the tragedy of a mutual friend who died in childbirth within a year of her marriage: « I shall always be contented and pleased, if it should please God that you never have to encounter this terrible risk... I own that children, from the consolation of their being yours, would be highly acceptable to me, if it were so appointed... I know I am already happy without them ». But that letter covered what must have been a deep pain for the two devoted lovers, for both John and Mary adored children.   However, the void was partly filled in 1775.

Mary's youngest brother George married and died young; but sadly his wife pre-deceased him and they left a young orphan girl of five years of age.   Elizabeth Catlett was adopted into the home at Olney vicarage.   Betsy's laughter rang through the modest rooms and out into the brick-walled garden.   John and Mary watched her with a growing parental pride.

This love for children revealed itself in Newton's care for the youngsters of Olney.   John Newton was a strong supporter of the Sunday School movement when it commenced in the 1780's under Robert Raikes.   This Gloucester journalist needed such help at a time when the Bishop of Rochester was preaching against him and the Archbishop of Canterbury was calling a conference of bishops to put an end to such work!   However, long before Raikes employed his four women at one shilling a day each to instruct the children of his Sunday School, John Newton could write of the one hundred children regularly attending his Thursday after-dinner meetings.   The Great House, owned by Lord Dartmouth and situated so conveniently to the church had fallen into disuse.   John applied to the Earl who arranged for it to be repaired, and the Great Room suited the purpose of these children's meetings.   Here John would meet his children, not to catechise them, though he intended to do that in due course, but so that he could « talk, preach, and reason with them, and explain the Scriptures to them in their own little way ».   The experiences of their pastor provided a never ending source of stories and illustrations and the children sat enthralled; they were equally delighted with the model ships he made out of paper. It was not long before the number rose to over two hundred and the captain marched his youthful army out of the Great House and into the chancel where they could muster with more space and comfort.

A YEAR OF REVIVAL

The year 1772 was perhaps the watershed of Newton's ministry at Olney. It would be wrong to assume that affairs declined immediately after this date, but certainly there was no greater year in his ministry before it.

The children's meetings increased and many of the young lives showed evident signs of a new spiritual vigour. The prayer meetings continued with unabated zeal and the Sunday evening gathering at the Great House was so crowded that Newton despaired of finding any way to limit the numbers. Gratefully he wrote to a friend: « It has been, and I hope still is, a time of grace and revival. I know not but we have had as many awakened within about three months past as for two or three years before », and these converts were progressing well in their faith. After the Sunday services the vestry was thronged with people seeking further help and this man, whose preaching fell far short of the standards set by the critics, was constantly assured of the help that his ministry had been to the Christians in his congregation. So warm were the people's prayers, so heartfelt their love and appreciation, that the old sea captain, who rarely shed a tear in the pulpit, often returned to the vicarage, sank into a deep sofa in the dining room and wept out his thankfulness to God.

Still the visitors came to the town, enquired for the vicarage and knocked at the heavy, panelled door. From January to May they were not free of visitors and John's admiration for the efficiency of Mary knew no bounds. When the last visitor left on May 14th, Newton recorded gratefully how many had been blessed under their roof. By July the stream of callers began once more.

The evident work of the Spirit was witnessed in the love and peace that existed amongst the members of the parish church; and this was itself a reflection of the firm but peaceable nature of the pastor. In a beautiful description of the Christians at Olney in 1768 John might well have been writing for 1772 also: « We are quiet and happy at Olney. We know nothing about disputes or divisions. If you pass a flock of sheep in a pasture towards evening, you may observe them all very busy in feeding. Perhaps here and there one may just raise his head and look at you for a moment, but down he stoops again to the grass directly. He cannot fill his belly by staring at strangers. Something in this way I hope it is with us. We care not who makes the noise, if we can get the grass. If they like *talking*, they may talk on; but we had rather *eat*. » And so John Newton fed his people, not with strife and dissension, but with the pure Word of God.

But it must never be imagined that the whole town was falling to the Gospel. Even in this year of « grace and revival » Newton found it necessary on Sunday, May 31st, to preach a sermon on Isaiah 58: 13-14, to encourage the town constables and magistrates, who had at last roused themselves to put a stop to the free abuse of the Lord's Day amongst many of the Olney inhabitants; and the very gospel that led some to Christ, for peace and forgiveness, hardened others in the town who became even more bold in their disobedience to the laws both of God and man. However, congregations grew until the church, chancel and belfry were nearly full and when a visiting evangelical clergyman arrived and the bell tolled to inform the town of a sermon, a congregation was never wanting.

CHAPTER 7.

A WIDER MINISTRY

Though John Newton was in charge of a parish church, he was by no means parochial. His ministry, like his mind, was large. Through his pen, his preaching, and his friendships, John demonstrated a love for the souls of all men, far and near. Long hours were spent in his study composing letters to distant enquirers, some of whom he would never meet, and few of whom would be added to his church. Days were eaten away by tiring journeys on horse or foot to reach a small and scattered community to whom he could preach a sermon, or to gather a lonely household of some distant farmstead around the winter's fire to listen to the Word of life. Newton's ministerial friendships were not narrow and rigid; his heart embraced all who loved the Truth. The despised dissenter and Methodist all found a place in his time and fellowship. To write of the true evangelical Gospel, to preach it anywhere and at any time, and to meet with those who did the same—these were his chief pleasures.

145

« MY CORRESPONDENCE IS SO LARGE »

On Saturday, November 17th, in the year of his settlement at Olney, Newton came to the end of a week of writing letters. It was not an unusual week for him, since letters poured into his home and John could often be found, for many hours a day, secluded in his study, hunched over his desk, and writing, writing, writing. But at the end of this particular week he wrote: « My leisure chiefly taken up this week with writing letters. Indeed my correspondence is so large that it almost engrosses my time (pulpit preparation excepted), and I know not well how to contract it ».

In 1774 he published many of these letters in his little book entitled *Omicron*. It was a selection of forty-one letters, full of practical advice and wise counsel. He wrote to a student of divinity urging him to apply himself to « the Holy Scriptures and prayer » as the chief means of attaining wisdom; to the enquiry as to how he should fill up his sermons, the young man was instructed to study people, for what he observed in any ten, he could be sure of in a thousand. In a letter, urging upon another correspondent the duty of family worship, John outlined not only the privilege and responsibility of this, but also the practical concerns of when and how: « You will, of course, choose those hours when you are least liable to be incommoded by the calls of business, and when the family can assemble with the most convenience ». Newton advised the reader not to leave it until late in the evening lest everyone would be too sleepy; in addition he urged husband and wife to pray together and for each other. John was convinced that family prayers would govern the life of the household; but he was not unsympathetic towards the man unused to these things and, remembering his own first faltering attempts at Liverpool, gave practical advice to overcome this obstacle. Newton had decided views of prayer and in a letter on « The Exercise of Social Prayer », he condemned long prayers: « It is better... that the hearers should wish the prayer had been longer, than spend half or a considerable part of the time in wishing it was over ». He also criticised prayers that give the promise of concluding and then start up again, and prayers that are little more than a sermon to the others present. John was equally opposed to that artificial voice which he detected in some of those who attended the Olney prayer meetings, and to the custom of « talking to the Lord with the voice they use upon the most familiar and trivial occasions ». When we are speaking to the King of kings, he concluded, there should be an air of seriousness and reverence about our prayer.

One who was about to engage in a controversy in which his cause was undoubtedly that of the truth, wisely applied to Newton for counsel. This Mr. Valiant for Truth was also valiant for peace and he at once saw the enquirer's weakness. John knew his correspondent to be on the side of right and a man of ability and, therefore, he was assured of certain victory, but « if you cannot be vanquished, you may be wounded ». He knew that the young man's « love of truth is joined with a natural warmth of temper » and the letter advised him how to view the opponent, the public, and himself in the contest. After wise counsel the curate of Olney concluded : « If we act in a wrong spirit, we shall bring little glory to God, do little good to our fellow-creatures, and procure neither honour nor comfort to ourselves.   If you can be content with showing your wit, and gaining the laugh on your side, you have an easy task; but I hope you have a far more noble aim... ».   Newton himself lived out the letter of this advice.

In a most valuable letter, « On hearing Sermons », John urged his reader to seek out a man whose ministry was not only acceptable but profitable. Once he had found such a man who preached the true evangelical Gospel he should « make a point of attending his ministry constantly ».   Newton had little time for those who run about after new preachers; they reminded him of Proverbs 27: 8: « As a bird that wandereth from her nest, so is the man that wandereth from his place ».   Such hearers « seldom thrive, they usually grow wise in their own conceits, have their heads filled with notions, acquire a dry, critical, and censorious spirit; and are more intent upon disputing who is the best preacher, than upon obtaining benefit to themselves from what they hear ».   Yet he warned also against becoming merely a hearer, and against hasty criticism of the minister: « It will be more useful for you who are a hearer, to consider whether the fault may not possibly be in yourself ».

In an age when smuggling was not only rife, but respectable, and everyone from prelate to pauper joined in the trade, Newton in a letter to « Professors in Trade » strongly condemned this « illicit commerce ». Even professing Christians justified their action; they claimed it was necessary to their livelihood to avoid the shilling tax on a pound of tea, and John demanded that if they persisted in their disobedience to the Law of God they should at least ensure that their practice would bear examination at their dying hour.

The pages of *Omicron* contained also devotional and doctrinal letters. In a letter on « Election and Perseverance » he unashamedly identified himself with the Reformers, and in a letter « On Union with Christ » he wrote of the Christian's « intimate, vital and inseparable union » with Christ. Three letters described three stages of the Christian's growth under the picture of the blade, the ear, and the full corn (A.B.C). A young man wrote to the author that he had found his own spiritual character aptly described in C and thanked him for it. He was somewhat disconcerted to receive a reply in which Newton apologised for omitting one essential feature of the Christian in the state of the full corn, namely, that he « never knew his own face ».

AROUND THE TOWN AND COUNTRY

Newton's preaching ministry was by no means limited to the plain wooden pulpit of the church of St. Peter and St. Paul. The fact that he was ungraceful in manner and unpolished in speech whilst preaching, seems hardly to have occurred to his rural congregations; they demanded his services everywhere. Two years after his settlement, John visited London where he preached fourteen times, and in August of that year he could write of his ministerial labours to Captain Clunie explaining that he had just completed six hours speaking both in church and home; and that was in Olney! During the summer months John toured the country with Mary, preaching

A wider ministry.

wherever he could find access in pulpit or cottage hearth. In 1767 they covered 650 miles and once managed to visit Howell Harris, the powerful Welsh evangelist.

Frequently, summer and winter, John would saddle his horse and ride off across filthy roads and rain-swept fields to a distant cottage where he would gather the poor folk around him and read, pray and expound the Scriptures so that even the ploughman and his son could understand. The clergyman would lead them in a hymn, accept their offer of a hot drink and a piece of hard coarse barley bread, warm his hands by the smoky fire and set off to another village. Typical was his entry into his diary for November 6th, 1764, when he walked to Denton (six miles from Olney), « and spent a few hours with a little knot of the Lord's people ».

One of John's favourite resorts was Lavendon Mill, where he would take tea with his friend Mr Perry, the miller, and afterwards preach to the congregation who had gathered in Mr. Perry's large barn. It very soon became a custom for Newton to spend the whole of the Friday of Whitsun week with the miller and his « church ».

When John arrived at Olney he determined to maintain a healthy relationship with all who preached the evangelical Gospel regardless of their denomination. He had lived with this mind until now and would continue to do so until his death. In spite of those strong Calvinistic doctrines of the sovereignty of God in predestination, which Newton so fearlessly preached, he confessed himself content to pray and work with anyone who did not swerve from the evangelical truths. What mattered for him was whether a man preached Christ crucified as the only sacrifice for sin, whether he insisted upon the necessity for the new birth by the Holy Spirit, and whether he proclaimed a living, vital Christian faith that should govern a man's life completely and conform him daily to the likeness of the eternal Son of God.

In consequence of this true evangelical spirit, the Rev. John Newton called upon the Rev. William Walker who had settled as pastor of the Baptist assembly in 1753. John went further, he was not ashamed to attend Mr. Walker's meeting place to listen to a sermon from William Grant of Wellingborough, and to dine with the good pastor. « I shall take this opportunity », John wrote in the July following his induction, « to set the door of acquaintance wide open. If they choose to keep it so, it is well, if not, I have but done my duty ». Happily the dissenters chose to keep it so.

The same regard held for the Rev. Mr Drake who, in the year 1759 came to watch over the flock meeting at the Independent chapel. On Tuesday, September 26th, 1765 John Newton cancelled his own prayer meeting so that he and his people could hear bold Mr Bradbury preach among the Independents. John wrote in his diary: « I am glad of such opportunities at times to discountenance bigotry and party spirit, and to set our dissenting brethren an example, which I think ought to be our practice towards all who love the Lord Jesus Christ and preach His Gospel without respect to forms or denominations ». When new pastors came to the Baptist and Independent chapels, Newton was there to welcome them. He expressed a longing to join the company of Olney Baptists who walked out of the village to attend the Baptist Association at Carlton in June 1774, but felt it wiser to remain at home, for his presence might offend. However, the following year the Association chose Olney as its meeting place and Newton took advantage of the opportunity by listening to the sermons and inviting a number of visiting ministers to lunch.

All this was much against the spirit of the times and Mary, with her cautious and conservative nature, and an even more conservative father, was not sure that she liked such fraternising. But John was adamant, and Mary showed her wisdom by trusting his.

« MR BULL IS YOUR POPE »

In the year that John Newton came to Olney, William Bull succeeded to the pastorate of the Independent chapel at Newport Pagnell. When the two men first met, they were not at once drawn to each other, perhaps because at times William lived up to his name. However, as time progressed, they were drawn more and more into each other's company. Apart from their denomination, they had everything in common. Like Newton, Bull was largely self-taught. He had learnt Hebrew with the sole aid of an old Bible with Hebrew letters heading the sections of the 119th Psalm, and he so mastered mathematics from a single copy of Whiston's *Mathematics*, that, as a teenager, he was contributing articles to the *Mathematical Magazine*. Latin and Greek soon followed. The two ministers met regularly, and Cowper would often discover them secluded in his Summer House and deep in serious discussion as each puffed at his pipe, which last activity the poet considered a foul practice. « Smoke-inhaling Bull, » as Cowper derisively called him, kept his pipe and pouch beneath the centre board of the Summer House.

William often preached at the Great House and John so consistently sought his counsel and exalted his wisdom that Mary teasingly rebuked him with the words, « I think Mr Bull is your pope ». In spite of this wifely deflation the last fourteen letters of *Cardiphonia* were addressed to John's « pope ». The relationship of the two men was both serious and lighthearted. Their differing views of church government and the Established Church led to long and profitable discussions between them. However they were both ready to share some point of humour together. Once when Newton was due to arrive in Newport Pagnell for the visit of a bishop, he sent his vestments ahead carefully addressed to the home of the Independent minister with the covering note: « herewith I send my sheep's clothing ».

THOMAS SCOTT

The curate-in-charge of the parishes of Ravenstone and Weston Underwood stalked into his study, slammed the door and threw himself down at his desk. If only that man Newton would keep to his own parish!

Thomas Scott was the son of a poor grazier. Ejected, for misconduct, from his apprenticeship to a physician, Thomas determined to apply for ordination, because in this path he would find an easier living than watching his father's sheep and cattle; there would be more leisure for reading and he would be able to distinguish himself as a literary man, which was his great ambition.

Accordingly, Scott taught himself Greek and Latin, satisfied his examiners, and was ordained into the Church of England in 1772. Scott was the opposite of all that evangelicalism stood for. He did not believe in the Trinity, denied that Christ was God manifest in the flesh, ridiculed the idea of Calvary as a substitution and covering for sin, rejected any thought of the need for regeneration by the Holy Spirit. What salvation was left after all this, he believed, could be earned by a life of good works. Not that Scott excelled at this point either! In twenty weeks Scott mastered Hebrew and spent most of his time in his study; his people were poor, ignorant and idle, but they saw very little of their clergyman unless they went to church, which, strangely, many of them did. Two years after his ordination Scott married. He had met his wife during a game of cards at which Thomas won all the stakes!

Living so close to Olney, it was inevitable that Scott should meet Newton sooner or later. That meeting took place in the year 1775 and immediately the two men entered into a lively discussion of doctrine. But Newton just would not argue; he was simple, direct and knew what he believed, but very courteous. Inquisitively Scott slipped into a pew at St. Peter and St. Paul to hear this strange man preach. To his

St. Peter and St. Paul's, Olney.

horror Newton gave out his text from Acts 13: 9,10: « Then Saul, (who also is called Paul) filled with the Holy Ghost, set his eyes on him, and said, O full of all subtilty and all mischief, thou child of the devil, thou enemy of all righteousness, wilt thou not cease to pervert the right ways of the Lord? » and Scott returned to his parish disgusted at the thought of a fellow clergyman preaching at him in this manner. Only later did Thomas Scott discover that Newton had no knowledge of his presence in the congregation that Sunday.

John Newton began a correspondence with Scott and took up, in great detail, all the points of doctrine upon which they differed. He shut himself away in the vicarage study and spent long hours carefully setting out the true Gospel, but he felt that little headway was gained. Scott was interested, and a little changed in his views, but by December 1775 he broke off the correspondence and returned to his cards and his books. Scott despised evangelicalism and the Methodist enthusiasts, and Newton represented both.

About the time he broke off corresponding with Newton, two of Scott's parishioners lay sick and dying in the cold poverty of their miserable cottage. Scott was too busy with his books even to notice their plight, until someone drew to his attention that the Rev. Mr Newton had frequently visited them and had brought comfort and cheer to the cheerless home. Scott was angered and yet rebuked. He threw himself into his study and thought once more about this man who had invaded his parish.

157

He might be contemptuous of Mr. Newton's doctrine, but he was forced to confess that the action of the curate at Olney was more consistent with the character of a minister than his own. Thomas Scott knelt before God in his study and asked forgiveness for his neglect of his duties. He at once visited the poor home of the dying parishioners and resolved to renew his acquaintance with Newton at the first opportunity.

During a time of personal distress Thomas Scott could think of only one man to whom he could turn. Accordingly, he visited Newton and received so much help and loving concern that it was not long before he found his views finally settled in the evangelical faith. In 1777, at the age of thirty, Thomas Scott became an evangelical, upset his vicar, lost many friends and sat down to publish his new beliefs and spiritual pilgrimage under the title, *The Force of Truth*. The young convert was soon preaching in Newton's pulpit.

When Newton left Olney, Scott, after a short interval, took his place in the vicarage and wrote and preached as a champion for the Truth. His mammoth « Family Bible », which was a commentary upon the whole Bible, was most valuable as a clear exposition of the Scriptures. It earned Scott little financial reward but became a spiritual treasure for many generations.

William Carey, the founder of modern missions, lived close to Olney and before Scott moved to the Lock Hospital and Mission in London in 1786, the young cobbler would often sit under his ministry. Carey wrote in 1821: « If there be anything of the Word of God in my soul, I owe much of it to Scott's preaching... » Carey may be thus rightly termed the spiritual grandchild of John Newton.

THE GREAT FIRE AND GUY FAWKES

John Newton was away in London. In 1776 a tumour on his thigh necessitated an operation which, in those days before anaesthetic, was a very painful experience. John had attended his physician at the appointed hour concluding: « I felt that being enabled to bear a very sharp operation, with tolerable calmness and confidence, was a greater favour granted to me than the deliverance from my malady ». He, who had frequently exhorted his frail wife to accept her weakness as God's loving chastisement, would not shirk the application himself. Within two weeks he was preaching for a friend in London.

He was away again in October 1777 when one of the thatched cottages caught alight. Before the people could empty their buckets onto the blaze, seven or eight homes were in flames. The inhabitants were virtually helpless and could do little more than watch the flames spread from roof to roof until twelve houses were destroyed and the whole town seemed threatened. Suddenly the wind changed, a gap in the row broke the fire's advance and the people of Olney set about damping the smouldering ruins and repairing the damage. Little was covered by insurance in this poor community and when Newton returned he wrote a hymn for the occasion and raised four hundred and fifty pounds through public subscriptions for the relief of his deprived people.

November 5th was always a dangerous day at Olney. Many of the youths were drunken and rowdy at the best of times but Guy Fawkes night was their excuse to be more wild than ever. As a result of the recent fire Newton, along with many leading towns-folk, considered it wise to put a stop to the usual orgy of festivities. Lighted candles set in the windows of thatched cottages and burning tapers carried drunkenly through the streets did not appear wise. The town was duly informed. But the mob thought otherwise.

John had seen the angry crowds before when they mobbed a flour wagon at times of hunger and soaring prices, but tonight it was a mob without cause or purpose and that was always more dangerous, for such a mob was inevitably unreasonable. The wild, lawless mob paraded the streets, breaking windows and demanding money from all they could seize. A messenger hammered upon the door of the vicarage and warned the incumbent that a group of forty or fifty drunken rowdies was approaching. John New-ton had harangued a crew into submission many times, and with a past like his there were few things left to make him tremble. (On his many lonely journeys it was only the insistence of Mary that hindered him from riding through the night.) John stood at the door of his vicarage ready to deal with the passionate gang. He had learned by long experience how a mob can be dealt with by recognising the leader and quietening him. But Mary was terrified, she sobbed and pleaded and fainted, and to calm his wife, « I was forced to send an embassy and beg peace. A soft message, and a shilling to the captain of the mob, secured his protection and we slept in safety. Alas, « tell it not in Gath! » I am ashamed of the story. »

There was a reason for the increasing lawlessness of the youth of Olney. In 1757 the Prime Minister, William Pitt, to meet the requirements of the Seven Years' War, greatly increased the size of the standing army and the militia. The militiamen were conscripted by ballot for a term of three years' service in Britain—a sort of Home Guard. The unrest in America which led to the War of Independence, began in the early 1770's. The increasing success of the American forces, especially after the young Frenchman La Fayette arrived to support them, forced the continuance of this militia ballot. Young men from Olney left the plough and the simplicity of village life and were educated in the school of profanity, gambling and drunkenness in His Majesty's Militia. Most of them enjoyed the life of comparative ease and returned to their quiet village dissatisfied with their lot. Cowper in his famous poem *The Task* wrote eloquently of the militia returned, and thus revealed the problems that faced the country curate. The young soldier now hated the plough and the field in which no drum or fife attended him, and longed for his smart comrades:

> « But with his clumsy port the wretch has lost
> His ignorance and harmless manners too.
> To swear, to game, to drink; to shew at home
> By lewdness, idleness, and sabbath-breach,

161

The great proficiency he made abroad,
T'astonish and to grieve his gazing friends,
To break some maiden's and his mother's heart,
To be a pest where he was useful once,
Are his sole aim, and all his glory now. »

Conscription ruined the youth of Olney and the sea captain waged a steady war for their restoration.

TIME TO MOVE

It was not merely the humiliation of treating with a drunken mob that troubled John; it was the fact that after thirteen years of tireless ministry and visitation amongst the two thousand inhabitants of Olney, such a mob could still be heard.

Many of that faithful, praying band that had warmly received the new curate in 1764 were now lying in the church-yard and he detected a loose indifference amongst the young people. He lamented that he « lived to bury the old crop on which any dependence could be placed ». By the end of the decade there was an observable thinning in the congregation and at times they could even dispense with the gallery. Fewer children attended his meetings. And John sadly noticed, that when the possibility of his removal to another parish had been mentioned to the prayer meeting, among all the warm and intimate prayers for him that followed none « put up one direct petition for my continuance ». Perhaps it was time to move.

Towards the end of 1779 John Thornton, who spent much of his time, and even more of his money, buying up the patronage of established churches and then filling the pulpits with evangelical men, offered Newton the living of St. Mary Woolnoth, Lombard Street, in the City of London. John and Mary felt it was right and Newton wrote facetiously to his old friend Bull : « My race at Olney is nearly finished. I am about to form a connection for life with one Mary Woolnoth, a reputed London saint in Lombard Street ».

On October 19th, 1781 the American War of Independence came to its successful conclusion, when General Cornwallis surrendered the British army to George Washington at Yorktown. Two years before Newton surrendered his parish with the same.sense of frustrated resignation. But John's grief and sense of failure when he left Olney were largely undeserved. He had made mistakes as every minister will. Perhaps at times his own spiritual battle conveyed itself to his parishioners; he was sufficiently honest to admit to a friend as far back as 1766 : « Coldness in prayer, and darkness, and formality in reading the Word are almost my continual burden. I want to be more lively, feeling and affectionate in spiritual things ». At another time he discovered himself visiting his people with a careless and indifferent heart. But, on the other hand, he was still visiting and he poured himself into the life of the parish. Hundreds owed their spiritual awakening to his preaching and pastoral care. His letters overflowed the Ouse and reached into the four corners of the country with rich spiritual advice. The town of Olney was fixed indelibly upon the map of English evangelical history. John had had many tempting offers to move before, to Hampstead, to Halifax, and even to become president of a new seminary in New England, but it had never been right. Now, however, was the time to move.

Before John accepted the call to London, he and Mary ran down the garden, through the hole in the wall at the end, across the lawn of Orchard Side and discussed the matter with William Cowper and Mrs Unwin. The sad eyes of Cowper scanned the serious face of his pastor; if any one had cause to be grateful for the public ministry and private counsel of John Newton, it was this « stricken deer ».

CHAPTER 8.

COWPER AND THE OLNEY HYMNS

A sallow, lean-faced young man bent over his writing table; the dreary dimness of his cramped apartment at the Inner Temple in the heart of eighteenth century London matched the despair and gloom of his mind. William Cowper picked up his pen and, comparing the summary judgement executed upon Judas with the lengthy turmoil of his own soul, referred to himself as « damned below Judas; more abhorred than he was » and continued:

> « Him the vindictive rod of angry justice
> Sent quick and howling to the centre head-long;
> I, fed with judgement, in a fleshly tomb, am
> Buried above ground. »

If ever the great poet had written his own epitaph, it is likely that his description of his life would have been displayed in those three dreadful words, « Buried above ground ».

A MOTHER'S LOVE

William Cowper was born on November 26th, 1731, in the Rectory at Berkhamsted, Hertfordshire and, apart from an inherited melancholy, events of the first eighteen years of his life combined to weigh heavily upon his spirits. Three brothers and two sisters all died in infancy or childhood and William was left with one brother, John, whose birth was the occasion of his mother's death, just two days before William's sixth birthday. Cowper's deep affection for his mother was reflected not only by the heart-broken child of six, but by the fact that forty-seven years later he could claim: « Not a week passes (perhaps I might with equal veracity say a day) in which I do not think of her ». At the age of fifty-eight, on receiving a miniature portrait of his mother, a very beautiful woman when she died at thirty-two years of age, the poet confessed that he wept, kissed it, and placed it where it would be the first and last object to catch his eye each day; he then wrote a poem of such warmth and feeling that it is hard to read it without strong emotion.

Cowper suffered throughout his life from a slight physical deformity of which few knew anything, but of which he was acutely sensitive. A lifelong weakness of his eyes was no small trouble to him and as late as 1781 he was writing « a slight disorder in my eye may possibly prevent my writing you a long letter ». Other incidents added to his melancholy. Along with the society of his day, Cowper would take a pleasant walk through Bedlam to seek amusement in the antics of the poor wretches caged there. A contemporary guide-book to London *Amusements Serious and Comical* described Bethlehem Hospital in Moorfields (Bedlam) as « a pleasant place... one entire amusement. Some were preaching, and others in full cry a-hunting; some were praying, others cursing and swearing; some were dancing, others groaning; some singing, others crying; and all in perfect confusion ». These « antics » had a greater effect upon the sensitive mind of the poet than upon most. A similar effect was produced when, one evening, as Cowper passed through a graveyard on his way home, the grave digger threw up a human skull that landed close by him!

His father obtained a place for him at Westminster City School, where he was a keen sportsman and a bright student and, after the expulsion of a bully, whom William feared so much that he came to recognise him only by his shoe buckles, he managed well enough. During one of his holidays a friend of the family committed suicide and his father showed him an article advocating self-destruction; he was intended to refute and despise it, but for such a mind as Cowper's it was an argument that lay like a seed awaiting the right time for germination.

INTO THE LAW

In 1749 Cowper left Westminster School and there followed what he himself described as « three years mis-spent in an attorney's office » in Holborn. He never enjoyed reading law and only sheer necessity forced him to take chambers in the Middle Temple in 1754. Here in the dinginess of the great city (he was always a country boy at heart) at a profession he increasingly hated, Cowper suffered a serious dejection of spirits. This malady was increased by a thwarted romance. Cowper had become greatly attached (perhaps love is not the word to use) to his cousin Theodora who lived at Southampton Row. During 1752 and 1753 the young couple saw each other daily and Cowper, who had already written a few boyish poems at Westminster, now set his pen moving seriously in the praise of Theodora. However, the young lady's father intervened and the relationship was summarily broken off in true eighteenth century filial obedience! Theodora never married and remained a constant admirer of the poet's rise to fame, frequently sending him anonymous gifts.

All these experiences, perhaps not uncommon for a young Georgian gentleman, combined to throw Cowper into a deep melancholy. A brief relationship with a young girl of sixteen, with whom there could be no possibility of marriage, and the tragic drowning of a close friend whilst bathing in the Thames, were hardly calculated to brighten his spirits.

ATTEMPTED SUICIDE

In 1757 the twenty-six years old lawyer moved to the Inner Temple where he continued for six gloomy years, almost certainly without a brief and hating the work and environment in which he was employed. By 1763 his financial position was desperate and, to another mind, the offer of the lucrative posts of Reading Clerk and Clerk of Committees in the House of Lords would have been gladly received. But Cowper, reluctant to face the public speaking this might entail asked for the less rewarding post of Clerk of the Journals of the House of Lords. Sadly his plan for obscurity was thwarted when he was ordered to prepare for a public examination to prove himself for this latter post. The possibility of appearing before the Lords to be examined was terrifying. Black despair blocked up his mind from study and frantically he awaited the dreadful ordeal: « A thought would sometimes come across my mind, that my sins had perhaps brought this distress upon me, that the hand of divine vengeance was in it; but in the pride of my heart I presently acquitted myself and thereby implicitly charged God with injustice, saying, What sins have I committed to deserve this? » A brief holiday by the sea proved to be no balm for a tortured mind and as the terrible day of examination approached, William Cowper contemplated suicide. The article handed to him by his father years before, a letter in his newspaper, a casual conversation in a public house, all led to one conclusion: « Perhaps there is no God, or if there be, the Scripture may be false? If so, then God has nowhere forbidden suicide. » He considered life as his own property and therefore at his own disposal. Cowper then fell into a pit, the slime of which was never erased from his mind—he deliberately set out to take his own life. He purchased a phial of laudanum, ordered a coach and set out for the Thames there to dispose of his sufferings. Laudanum was a solution of opium and wine, commonly used to deaden pain, but in larger doses it would kill. Yet Cowper felt an invisible Hand restrain his own and he could not bring the phial to his lips.   In disgust and despair he returned to his meagre lodgings.   Within the safety of his rooms he resorted to a pen-knife but the blade snapped and he threw it to the floor.   He tried to hang himself but the weight of his body broke first an iron pin and then a wooden spar.   The third attempt was almost successful, but just as he lost consciousness the garter he used as a noose tore apart and his body slumped to the floor.   William Cowper, who could succeed neither in romance nor law, could not succeed in taking his own life either.   He felt doomed to be « buried above ground ».

The post offered him in the Lords was withdrawn and Cowper, with friends and relatives trying vainly to console his fevered mind, was introduced, for the first time, to an evangelical Christian in the person of Martin Madan.   Cowper had heard of his cousin Madan and had long dismissed him as an enthusiast; he was a leader among the evangelicals and this fact alone was sufficient reason to bring him into contempt in Georgian society.   But as Madan sat by his bedside, William Cowper heard for the first time of the atoning suffering of the blood of Christ, of His righteousness for our salvation, of the free offer of pardon and the urgent need of repentance and faith in Christ.   These conversations brought only a temporary respite and soon Cowper became seriously deranged in his mind.

DR. COTTON'S ASYLUM

In December 1763 the pathetic form of this young lawyer arrived at a private asylum in St. Albans cared for by Dr Nathaniel Cotton, himself an evangelical Christian. Here Cowper went through a period of intense mental agony and for a period of seven terrible months a conviction of sin and an expectation of imminent judgement never left him. A snatch of one of his poems plainly reveals his state of mind at this time:

> « Then, what soul distressing noises
> Seemed to reach me from below,
> Visionary scenes and voices
> Flames of hell and screams of woe! »

During the early summer of 1764 Cowper picked up a Bible; it was not his own, for all his books were dispersed when he left the Inner Temple and, even at the height of his literary fame, his personal library did not consist of more than a dozen books! He read the story of the raising of Lazarus, and later wrote of his reaction: « I saw so much benevolence, mercy, goodness and sympathy with miserable man, in our Saviour's conduct, that I almost shed tears ». William longed for peace but felt he had rejected the Redeemer and had forfeited all His favour. A short time afterwards, whilst walking in the garden, Cowper idly opened a Bible that he found lying on a bench and read from Romans 3:25 concerning Christ: « Whom God hath set forth to be a propitiation through faith in His blood, to declare His righteousness for the remission of sins that are past, through the forbearance of God ». His response was immediate: « I saw the suffering of the atonement He had made, my pardon sealed in His blood, and all the fulness and completeness of His justification ». With an unspeakable joy he threw himself before God and embraced his new-found Saviour. Cowper picked up his pen to express his pilgrimage:

> « Me, through waves of deep affliction,
> Dearest Saviour, Thou hast brought,
> Fiery deeps of sharp conviction
> Hard to bear and passing thought,
> Sweet the sound of grace divine
> Sweet the grace which makes me thine. »

By June 1765 Cowper was well enough to leave St. Albans and, after a short stay with his brother at Foxton, he removed to lodgings in Huntingdon. Still a reserved and retiring young man, Cowper was pleased with the offer of friendship from William Unwin who introduced him to his parents and his sister Susanna. It was not long before Cowper moved in as a lodger in this decidedly evangelical home and heartily embraced their disciplined life of piety. Shortly after his arrival in the Unwin home the whole family began to read *An Authentic Narrative* and they longed to meet this man Newton who had known such a singular experience of God. Cowper longed to meet Newton also, but meanwhile the *Narrative* inspired him to write the story of his own spiritual life to the year of his arrival in Huntingdon. Someone placed in his hands a copy of Doddridge's *Rise and Progress of Religion in the Soul* and Cowper spent many pleasant days sitting in the quiet garden and learning the privileges and challenge of his new faith.

Early in the spring of 1767 Mr Unwin was thrown from his horse, broke his skull and died a few days after. The household was thrown into a grief only lightened by the hope of a life to come. Meanwhile, unknown to the family, John and Mary Newton were returning from a long and wearisome tour of the country. John had preached much and was looking forward to returning to his people at Olney when the chaise broke down; Mary was slightly injured and the couple were forced to accept the warm hospitality of Dr. Conyers, a brother-in-law to John Thornton. Dr. Conyers knew of the Unwins but not of Mr Unwin's death and urged Newton to visit the family. Accordingly John and Mary arrived at the home a few days after the funeral. The comfort and advice offered by their new friend, his interest in their welfare, and, above all, his clear evangelical faith settled the issue. Mrs Unwin, the two children and the lodger visited Olney and fell in love with the preacher, the people and the place; they were all « sick of the spiritless and unedifying ministry at Huntingdon » and so arranged to rent a house in the quiet Buckinghamshire town.

ORCHARD SIDE

On August 14th, 1767 the occupants of the Olney Vicarage received four more visitors who stayed until Orchard Side was decorated; however it was not long before the guests moved into Orchard Side, and for the next nineteen years Cowper lived here with the Unwins, until William and Susanna left home to marry. William Unwin, contemplating the large stone and brick building, once referred to it as « the Prison ».

The Vicarage stood with its back to the village and Orchard Side turned its back to the Vicarage, but behind their front doors a well-worn path, a few stone steps and a hole in the wall linked the two dwellings. William Cowper, or Cooper as John Newton rightly knew him, became a regular visitor at the back door by which he would let himself in and slip up the two flights of wide stairs to the pastor's study.

Mrs Unwin was seven years senior to Cowper but she cared for him as a son and, at least while William and Susanna lived at home, few thought it strange that Cowper should remain in the home after the death of her husband. In December 1769 Mrs Unwin, for whom Cowper always had a deep and respectable affection, fell ill and the pain that this occasioned in him led directly to the writing of the beautiful hymn: « Oh for a closer walk with God ».

This hymn was composed on December 9th and 10th, and although his « dearest idol » was soon restored to health, Cowper had already learnt that experiences can often make the Lord seem distant to the Christian. The second verse was a cry from his heart:

> « Where is the blessedness I knew,
> When first I saw the Lord?
> Where is the soul-refreshing view
> Of Jesus, and his word? »

But having, in verse five, torn his dearest idol from its throne to worship only God, the poet could confidently conclude:

> « So shall my walk be close with God,
> Calm and serene my frame;
> So purer light shall mark the road
> That leads me to the Lamb. »

Cowper's love for Mary Unwin, though passionately expressed in some of his poems, was never of the kind he had for Theodora. There was never anything remotely improper in the relationship of William and Mary; and Newton, cast in the strict Puritan mould of uprightness, never questioned Mrs Unwin's relationship with his poor, sick friend.

Cowper entered enthusiastically into the labours of John Newton, assisting him at all times and rarely allowing a day to pass without fellowship with his pastor. He helped to teach the children, rode out with Newton on his preaching visits to neighbouring villages, and led many of the prayer meetings in the town. John Newton helped Cowper to overcome his diffidence in praying publicly and it was not long before William's voice could be heard at most of the prayer meetings; one who heard him many times remarked: « Of all the men I ever heard pray, no one equalled Mr Cowper ». Newton valued these prayers immensely; when Cowper prayed it seemed that he saw the Lord whom he addressed, face to face. The shepherd at Olney equally valued his young friend's company and assistance. William Cowper became as familiar a figure in the town as the pastor himself and the poor lace-makers and farmers always valued a conversation with the frail, poet. For a few years William was very happy in his work.

OLNEY HYMNS

John was already writing hymns when William arrived in Olney, and the poet gladly added his own compositions to the growing store available to the Sunday and Tuesday congregations. The gift that the blasphemous sailor had once turned into ribald and profane verse was now employed for the glory of God. John was well aware of the value of those *Divine and Moral Songs* of old Dr Watts. Their words he could never quite dismiss from his mind, even in his most degenerate days. The cottagers at Olney were used to simple songs and if they sung their Lace Tells all day, why not spiritual songs in the evening?

By 1779 Newton and Cowper were able to produce a little hymn book entitled *The Olney Hymns*. Two hundred and eighty hymns came from the curate and sixty-eight from the poet, but if the latter lost the race in quantity he excelled in quality. The first edition cost two shillings and six pence for a bound copy and was divided into three sections: « On texts of Scripture », « On Occasional Subjects » and « On the Progress and Changes of the Spiritual Life ». Those which belonged to Cowper were prefixed with the letter C. Not only was it more convenient for the

176

Olney people to have the hymns collected in one book, but John had cause to protest that of the hymns that fled into the outside world many were claimed as the product of those who had no part in their origin.

The more serious reasons for publication John also gave in his preface. It was a monument, he considered, « to perpetuate the remembrance of an intimate and endeared friendship ». He complained that it was only his friend's illness that limited his valuable contribution. He and Cowper wrote for the poor parishioners of Olney and thus, Newton declared, he would not apologise for the simplicity and sometimes coarseness of his own poetry. Likewise he claimed for his hymns a doctrine that well expressed his beliefs and he could withdraw nothing. « The hour is approaching, and at my time of life cannot be very distant,» concluded Newton who had another thirty-eight years to run, « when my heart, my pen and my tongue will no longer be able to move in the service of the people of God ».

Among Newton's contributions was his most famous hymn « Amazing Grace ». This hymn was based upon 1 Chronicles 17:16,17 where King David reviewed the mercy of God to a man as weak and sinful as himself. John Newton reviewed his own life:

> « Amazing grace! (how sweet the sound!)
> That saved a wretch like me!
> I once was lost, but now am found;
> Was blind, but now I see.

'Twas grace that taught my heart to fear,
And grace my fears relieved;
How precious did that grace appear,
The hour I first believed! »

« Grace », for John Newton, was the undeserved mercy of God upon his sinful and rebellious life. And thus he continued into verse three:

« Through many dangers, toils, and snares,
I have already come;
'Tis grace has brought me safe thus far,
And grace will lead me home. »

It is sad to note that few hymn books today include Newton's final verse to this grand hymn. The substitute, « When we've been there a thousand years... » is much inferior to Newton's:

« The earth shall soon dissolve like snow,
The sun forbear to shine;
But God, who called me here below,
Will be for ever mine. »

Other hymns reflected his old sea-faring life; like « Though troubles assail and dangers affright ». Written in February 1773 this hymn originally contained a third verse:

« We may, like the ships,
By tempests be tost
On perilous deeps,
But cannot be lost:

Though Satan enrages
The wind and the tide,
The promise engages
The Lord will provide. »

Newton had long experience of the truth of this hymn! Similarly another hymn began with a verse the words of which must have taken his memory back to many violent days at sea, and particularly to that terrible storm in 1748:

« Begone, unbelief,
My Saviour is near,
And for my relief
Will surely appear:
By prayer let me wrestle,
And He will perform;
With Christ in the vessel,
I smile at the storm. »

John Newton is particularly noted for his hymn about the Christian Church:

« Glorious things of thee are spoken,
Zion, city of our God! »

How accurately the closing lines echoed his own experience:

« Fading is the worldling's pleasure,
All his boasted pomp and show;
Solid joys and lasting treasure,
None but Zion's children know. »

179

Another warmly sincere hymn is contained in the words of one commencing:

« How sweet the name of Jesus sounds
In a believer's ear! »

For a time Newton wrote a new hymn for his prayer meeting each week and frequently expounded it before his congregation were permitted to sing it for the first time. Many of his hymns were topical; the great fire in 1777 and even the visit of a lion to the town provided him with material for a hymn!

William Cowper's contribution included « Jesus! where'er Thy people meet », « Hark, my soul! it is the Lord », « There is a fountain filled with blood », and « Sometimes a light surprises the Christian while he sings ».

This last hymn reflects the many occasions when the poet slipped into his own, high-backed, wooden pew in the parish church and felt the deep sadness of his heart lifted into praise as his pastor led the service and entered energetically into the preaching of the Word of God:

« Sometimes a light surprises
The Christian while he sings;
It is the Lord who rises
With healing in His wings. »

These hymns confirmed for posterity his deep and sincere evangelical faith, however storm-tossed it was to become.

HIS OLD GLOOM

Towards the end of 1770 Cowper fell back into his old gloom and Newton, alarmed at the prospect, encouraged him to write more hymns. « God moves in a mysterious way » was written at the beginning of this second period of melancholy and William held on to the truth that « God is His own interpreter and He will make it plain ». During a solitary walk on a cold January day Cowper felt a warning of his approaching distress and set down this hymn.

Two years later Susanna moved away from Orchard Side to marry (her brother having moved earlier) and, to avoid improper speculation, William Cowper and Mrs Unwin engaged to marry. She was forty-eight and he was forty-one. Sadly his deeper depression which began in January 1773 frustrated this plan; almost certainly it was hastened by the plan itself. Cowper once more found himself in the terrible grip of depression that threw him ever deeper into despair. One month after he entered this dark tunnel, which ended only in death, Cowper had a dream in which a « Word » was given to him. He never revealed this message but for ever considered it was the death knell of his hope and confidence in Christ. In 1784 he wrote of his dream: « The latter end of next month will complete a period of eleven years, in which I have spoken no other language (than despair). It is a long time for a man, whose eyes were once opened, to spend in darkness; long enough to make despair an inveterate habit, and such it is with me. » He later added that « all consolation vanished at that time ».

Cowper rarely again attended public worship; he shunned the company and activities he once loved so much; his conversation steered carefully away from evangelical subjects and his pen, though yet to win him great fame as a national poet, never again moved across the page with expressions of Christian experience and worship to lead the congregation at Olney, (with one exception in 1788 when he was prevailed upon to write a hymn for the Sunday School). Cowper maintained a warm relationship with Newton and they corresponded frequently after Newton's removal to London but his letters became almost void of references to his soul or his Saviour; all that remained were such fragments as: « We think of you often, and one of us (Mrs Unwin) prays for you; the other will when he can pray for himself ».

It is often claimed that this lapse into soul despair, was the means of the liberation of his latent gifts as a poet; he was now free to range his mind and talent over the whole canvas of life and experience rather than be hedged within the narrow confines of the evangelical faith. It is certainly true that but for the circumstances of this tragic depression Cowper might never have become such a star among the poets, but we may well ask whether the absence of more hymns that undoubtedly would have come from his pen, and the subsequent black despair, that he once referred to as « the belly of this hell », under which he worked until his death twenty-seven years later, was not too high and tragic a price to pay for renown. John and Mary cared for him and watched over him with an untiring love. Many times John was called out at night and, slipping his great coat on his shoulders, would hurry to bring comfort to the tortured mind of « Sir William » as he affectionately called him. On April 12th, 1773, Cowper moved to the Vicarage for a few days; John and Mary Newton cared for him here with selfless devotion for the next fourteen months!

Newton was prepared to weather the criticisms that faced him. Many who did not know the poet well, considered it most improper for Cowper and Mrs Unwin to live in the same house. In fact it was a perfectly innocent relationship and John and Mary knew this. However the gossips seized on the scandal and even John Thornton indicated his disgust at Newton actually bringing them into his own home. But John, adamant that he was doing right by his poor friend, stood firm, and the storm blew over.

But there was little hope left for the man who considered himself sentenced to a state of « desertion and perpetual misery ». He believed everyone hated him, and that his food was poisoned. By the end of the following year he had made a little progress, sufficient to return to his own house with Mrs. Unwin. His days were spent writing, gardening and caring for his ever growing menagerie. At one time Cowper possessed five rabbits, three hares (Puss, Tiny and Bess), two guinea pigs, a magpie, a jay, a starling, two goldfinches, two canaries, two dogs, a squirrel and a cat. Cowper had earlier emptied his garden shed of flowers and he now spent hours there writing. Many of his letters are quaintly addressed from « The Greenhouse ».

THE RISE TO FAME

When John and Mary Newton came into the parlour at Orchard Side, Cowper and Mrs Unwin felt ill at ease; they knew something was wrong. Newton sat down and gently unfolded the story of his call to St. Mary Woolnoth's in London. The poet's heart

Lady Austen, Mary Unwin and Cowper

sank and his mind screamed alarm, but kindly and rather pathetically he agreed to the wisdom of the move, made suitable expressions of gratitude for past friendship and drank tea with his friends. Soon the Newtons moved. Cowper felt bereft of a very dear friend. He would walk out into his garden and watch the smoke rising from the study chimney at the Vicarage and remember the days when it signified that Mr Newton was at his desk and the poet could slip quietly in for a few moments prayer and conversation, but now, though the walls had not changed their appearance and the bolt of the door sounded as it always had and the gate still creaked on its hinges, Cowper felt alone and helpless. He turned to William Bull from whom, tobacco and smoke excepted, he gained much help.

The following year Lady Austen entered the life of Orchard Side. It was to this energetic and lively lady, for whom Cowper clearly had a reciprocated infatuation, that the poet owed much of his fame. His two greatest poems, *John Gilpin* and *The Task*, are directly attributable to her inspiration. However Cowper, aware of his true feelings for Lady Austen, abruptly concluded their association in deference to his regard for Mrs Unwin. Cowper's poems and prose were eagerly sought by an avid public and the honours and flattery of eminent people poured into Weston Underwood, the home on the estate of Sir John and Lady Throckmorton, to which he and Mrs Unwin moved in 1786. Here he began his translation of Homer.

But with all his steady rise to fame, and his work appeared frequently in the Metropolis, Cowper could never escape his fearful dream: « Prove to me that I have a right to pray » he would demand « and I will pray without ceasing... but let me add, there is no encouragement in the Scripture so comprehensive as to include my case, nor any consolation so effectual as to reach it... I have not asked a blessing upon my food these ten years, nor do I expect that I shall ever ask it again. »

185

Letters arrived regularly from the city of London, and William Cowper waited eagerly for the sound of Dick Tyrell and his « twanging horn » that heralded the arrival of the post. Newton always had words to suit the occasion and warmly commended every new literary venture of his friend. Letters from John and Mary could be light and cheerful or serious and encouraging as suited the poet's need. Newton grieved over Cowper's darkness more than all, but his belief in an eternal salvation was unshaken and, rightly, John never doubted Cowper's ultimate acceptance with God, even when the poet himself most certainly did.

William's life, serious writing excepted, became a round of elegant trifling; he altered his garden landscape because his neighbours had, and sowed his seeds with meticulous care and tended his potplants with an almost paternal interest. He took long walks into the surrounding countryside and summer and winter alike found him pacing the lanes and fields; but his life was enclosed and withdrawn. At times he would talk freely with those he met, but on other occasions he would pass by, lost in his own sad world of dreams, voices and despair.

In a letter to Mrs Newton, acknowledging the receipt of a gift of fish, to which Cowper was very partial, he wrote of John's visit to Ramsgate and recalled Newton's seafaring life and the memories the sight of the ocean would doubtless recall; with an obvious reference to himself he continued: « There are some for whom it would be better to be swallowed up in the deeps of the ocean, than to sit scribbling quietly and at their ease as I do. Yet it is so natural to shrink back from the thoughts of eternity, I know my days are prolonged not in mercy but in judgement. » After Newton's safe return to London from this journey to the sea, Cowper wrote to his friend:

> « Your sea of trouble you have passed
> And found the peaceful shore;
> I, tempest toss'd, and wrecked at last,
> Come home to port no more. »

Yet throughout his mental torment Cowper never doubted the truth and value of the atonement of Christ; indeed, he admitted the free forgiveness of God's pardoning love « to every case except my own ». In 1785 he could write: « Thy forgiveness is large and absolute ». *The Task*, written a year earlier, contains these lines at the close of Book V:

> « But, O Thou bounteous Giver of all good!
> Thou art of all Thy gifts Thyself the crown!
> Give what Thou canst, without Thee we are poor;
> And with Thee rich, take what Thou wilt away. »

It was the experience of applying all these truths to himself that Cowper could never again acquire after 1773.

To his melancholic mind the poet now added a hypochondriac concern for his health. Fresh air and exercise were accompanied by liberal consultations with various physicians and more liberal applications of soluble tartar for indigestion; a flesh brush for

187

lumbago, bark to remove headaches, laudanum to cure insomnia and Elliott's medicine for his eyes; his own electrotherapy machine was added for good measure! Sadly, the only spiritual advice Cowper sought at this time, with the exception of his regular correspondence with John in London, was from Mr Teedon, the eccentric old schoolmaster who considered himself God's gift to counsel the poet. Teedon was as self-assured as Cowper was self-condemned. He interpreted his admirer's many dreams, always favourably, and « advised » him in his great decisions. It is sad to observe such a great mind influenced by such a small one. In Newton, Cowper possessed a far wiser and more mature counsellor.

In December 1791 Mrs Unwin was seized by a sudden stroke and, though she recovered from the resulting partial paralysis, was never again fully fit. Her illness was a great trial to Cowper. His last and only rock of defence against the mental storms was being slowly eroded from his life. Throughout his deepest distress, his sullen silences, his attempted suicides, Mrs Unwin cared for the poet with a sympathy and affection that made her a silent heroine. In the autumn of 1793, as her life ebbed slowly away, he wrote a pathetically exquisite eulogy, *My Mary*.

Before his death one ray of light flitted briefly into his life. It happened on Sunday, October 16th, 1792. Cowper, Mrs Unwin and a cousin were walking in an orchard when he found himself able to approach God in prayer. « I prayed silently for everything that lay nearest to my heart, with a considerable degree of liberty... The next morning I was favoured with that spiritual freedom to make my requests known to God; I have enjoyed some quiet, though not uninterrupted by threatenings of the enemy. » However, it was only a fleeting glimpse of the sun between the clouds and the man, who had « three threads of despondency for one of hope », was writing in 1793, « I believe myself the only instance of a man to whom God will promise everything and perform nothing ».

THE MOVE TO DEREHAM

By 1795 Mary was deteriorating physically as rapidly as William deteriorated mentally. In July, his cousin « Johnny » Johnson, prevailed upon them to move to Norfolk and settle near his own parish at East Dereham. Cowper and Mrs Unwin accordingly took up their residence in the untenanted parsonage at North Tuddenham. The move provided no cure, and the poet's dismal frame of mind continued.

Johnson encouraged a move inland and settled the ailing couple at Dunham Lodge near Swaffham in October 1795. However, since this placed « Johnny » at least 15 miles from the scene of his ministry and necessitated his absence for the whole of Sunday, they later moved to Dereham. Dereham, with its 2,500 inhabitants, was in the centre of Norfolk and its long and interesting history, together with the attractiveness of the surrounding countryside, made it an agreeable enough place for Cowper.

THE STRICKEN DEER

On December 17th, 1796 Mary Unwin died. Cowper accompanied Johnson upstairs and gazed at the now relaxed and peaceful face of the only person for whom he experienced such constant affection. After a few minutes he threw himself into the corner of the room with a cry of despair; he then became more composed and never referred to Mary or mentioned her name from that day to the end of his life. She was buried at night according to custom and to avoid his knowledge.

Cowper's « voices » continued with increasing vengeance. Convinced that on his bed he was assailed by good and evil spirits, of which the latter invariably gained mastery, he now wrote with the pen of misery dipped in the deepest despair. In August 1798 the poet resumed his revision of Homer (« I may as well do this for I can do nothing else ») which he completed in the following March. Cowper felt he had nothing left to wish, but the wish of many years, that he had never existed.

On March 20th 1799 this « stricken deer » as he once called himself, wrote one of his last poems, *The Castaway*. It is the story of a poor seaman who was swept overboard in a storm. He battled against the waves, and his companions, hearing his cry, threw casks and corks overboard in a futile attempt to save him. Finally the sailor succumbed and fell beneath the waves. It was a parable of his life:

« But misery still delights to trace
It's semblance in another case
No voice divine the storm allay'd
No light propitious shone;
When, snatch'd from all effectual aid
We perished, each alone,
But I beneath a rougher sea,
And 'whelmed in deeper gulf than he. »

As Cowper began to sink from life a friend one day asked him how he felt. « Feel! » he replied, « I feel unutterable despair! » William Cowper died on Friday, 25th April 1800 in his 69th year and was buried at East Dereham Church beside Mary Unwin. As a memorial to a friend he loved and admired, John Newton took up his pen to write a short biography of Cowper's life, but ill-health and his own death intervened.

A popular biography of Cowper, written by Lord David Cecil in 1929, laid most of the blame for Cowper's sad derangement at the door of Newton and his evangelical faith. Cecil described Newton as « narrow and uncouth... clumsy, careless, insensitive and tactless », and his letters as « crude and absurd ». For good measure Lord Cecil accused Newton of an « indecent and ridiculous » application of his creed, adding, « nothing could persuade him not to thrust his views down your throat ». One is tempted to wonder if Lord David had read the story of someone else by mistake. The love and care of John and Mary for William and Mary is as touching as it was sincere. Cowper had no greater or more understanding friend, and the poet never tired of declaring this. If

John Newton's fault lay anywhere it was in his kind gentleness of spirit and his avoidance of all unnecessary controversy.

Certainly Cowper never blamed his evangelical faith for his depression. An inherited mental imbalance, a physical deformity and a natural melancholic disposition all contributed to a state that denied him the enjoyment of the blessings that were rightly his as a child of God. But for his Christian faith it is doubtful whether Cowper would ever have lived to become a poet of renown; his residence in St. Albans would have been his last.

The story of William Cowper is the most tragic of all our hymn writers. It was his lot to experience the truth referred to by the old divines: « God sometimes puts His children to bed in the dark ». Johnny Johnson remarked that at his death « the expression with which his countenance had settled was that of calmness and composure mingled, as it were, with holy surprise ». This expression reflected his present state, for William Cowper had gazed upon the full light of the face of the Sun of Righteousness in that place where there is no more sorrow or darkness and he had learnt the true meaning of his hymn:

> « Then in a nobler, sweeter song
> I'll sing Thy power to save,
> When this poor lisping, stammering tongue
> Lies silent in the grave. »

CHAPTER 9.

LONDON 1780

John Newton had not chosen a pleasant year to set up home in London. Although he did not leave Olney until January, on December 19th, 1779, he preached his first sermon at St. Mary Woolnoth's from Ephesians 4:15, « Speaking the truth in love ». Six months later on Friday, June 2nd, 1780 « Sir Mob » poured into the streets of London and rampaged through the city with unchecked fury.

London was no stranger to the rule of the mob for with a population of just under one million there was no organised police force. The total number of constables, peace officers, watchmen and patrols amounted to a little over three thousand men, but many were only part time; large numbers were old and only in employ to keep them out of the workhouse or « off the parish », and there were few who were not open to bribes. The Lord Mayor could hardly expect to employ fit and capable men for only eight shillings a week. The watchmen, or « Charlies », were given a lamp, a rattle, a stick, and a box to shelter in. « Charley » became the butt of everyone's humour and youthful gangs employed their evenings by turning

193

his little wooden box to face the wall so that he could not get out until the morning.

To protect themselves the citizens formed « mug-houses » at certain taverns from which they would sally forth armed with clubs and cudgels whenever a section of the mob became threatening. No day would pass without vicious street quarrels ending in surly, blood-letting affrays. To the new clergyman, it was not unlike the West Coast of Africa! The trades-men would riot for cause or no cause and the sailors, the silk-weavers, the colliers, and the hat-dyers had all turned into Sir Mob as occasion demanded. But of all the riots in the eighteenth century, none were to be compared with the Gordon Riots of June 1780.

John Newton had not long found himself a home in Charles Square, Hoxton, and was waiting for Mary and Betsy to join him. It was a pleasant enough dwelling with « green trees in front, and a green field backwards, with cows feeding in it, so that it has some little resemblance of the country ». He entered enthusiastically into his labours in the Metropolis.

LORD GORDON AND SIR MOB

In 1778 George Saville had introduced a Bill into Parliament that proposed restoring many privileges to the Roman Catholics. Since the death of Queen Anne and her Catholic inspired Schism Bill on August 1st, 1714, their fortunes had reversed, and Rome felt unwanted. Saville's timing was perfect.

Most of the Members were out of town and the Bill passed easily through the slender House. But the nation protested and Lord Gordon, a fanatical Scottish M.P., declared he would come to London with one hundred and eighty thousand men at his back and petitions to reach from the Speaker's chair to the central windows of Whitehall. In the event, on June 2nd, Gordon rallied between sixty thousand to eighty thousand people (Newton preferred to call it « upwards of fifty thousand persons ») in St. George's Field, harangued them with reminders of papal intolerance and the fires of Smithfield, and marched them, six abreast, into the city. With cries of « No Popery » they poured across the newly built Blackfriars Bridge, ignored the half-penny toll, surrounded the Houses of Parliament and threatened to murder the honourable Members. The scene was one of utter confusion as Members, sword in hand, promised first to kill Lord Gordon, who was trying to address the House, and then to defend the liberty of the House with their lives. Lords and bishops were hustled and roughed and on Friday the mob spilled into the streets and alleys of the city and began what the new rector called « those cruel devastations ».

John wrote at length describing in great detail the events that followed; events that dwarfed the Olney riots by comparison. He could not avoid being an eye-witness, for on Saturday the crowd surged into Hoxton and destroyed a Catholic School which had been opened in response to the Act of 1778.

A brief respite followed on Sunday, but this was hardly due to a religious conscience for, as John was at pains to emphasise, the riots were not supported by the Protestant Association, but « by a set of idle people of no religion at all ».   Many among the wild and reckless hordes who would gladly have died (and did) for « No Popery », hardly knew whether the Pope was man or beast.

The violence returned to the streets throughout Monday, and on Tuesday troops were stationed at the Tower, Parliament and other strategic places, but since they were under orders not to fire their presence only increased the farce of law and order; the crowds actually spat on the soldiers and pulled their noses!   By the evening the city was in the hands of Sir Mob.   Newgate and New Prison were set on fire and the prisoners released; Lord Mansfield's library of irreplaceable manuscripts was gutted and scores of homes were fired.   The drunken, brawling rioters roamed the streets looting, firing and beating.   Innocent people were « arrested » or dragged from their homes and ordered to pay fines in default of which their homes were destroyed, together with what Newton gravely called: « other acts of cruelty too shocking to mention ».

On Wednesday, which John considered to be the worst day of all, the violence reached its crescendo.   Every prison in London, with one exception, was burnt and the inmates set free; a distillery at Holborn was destroyed and whilst some of the rioters perished in the flames others literally drank themselves to death by lapping the neat spirit that trickled down the gutter.   The Bank, close by St. Mary's, was assaulted and a detachment of soldiers repulsed the

196

mob « with much slaughter ».   What John did not see was that terrified Jews put up notices declaring: « This house is a Protestant » and one Italian touched the spirit of the riot by chalking on his bolted door, « No Religion »!

At last, on Wednesday evening, the king ordered out the Guards, and the reassuring rattle of musketry lulled John to sleep.   On Thursday morning the city woke up to the debris of the previous week's carnage: smouldering homes, a pall of smoke, half-burned bonfires, broken casks and bottles and over two-hundred bodies lying in the streets.   The troops marched and rode through the city, the firemen brought out their hoses, the shutters nervously opened for a show of business and the inhabitants awoke from their nightmare. Twenty-eight rioters were executed, thirty-one were transported for life, and the Rev John Newton returned to his vestry, re-commenced his visitation and wrote reassuringly in the margin of his letter, « We are well ».

The following Sunday Newton announced his morning text from Lamentations 3: 22, « It is of the Lord's mercy we are not consumed » and in the evening he preached from Psalm 46: 10, « Be still, and know that I am God ».

STREETS AND NOISE

The city to which the Newtons came in 1780 was one of noise, filth, violence and extravagance.   Certainly

197

the inhabitants were pleasantly surrounded by those « green fields with cows », and Chelsea, Hyde Park, Paddington, Tottenham Court, Islington (one of the most beautiful of English villages), Hoxton, Bethnal Green, Mile End and Stepney, formed a green-belt of fields and farms around the city. On the south side of the Thames, Camberwell was a leafy grove, Herne Hill was a park set with stately trees and Denmark Hill to Norwood was one wooded wild.

But the streets of London were generally narrow, unpaved and ill-lit. There were few pavements and a line of posts protected the pathway from the ugly wheels of the carriage. Even this pathway was negotiated slowly and painfully, for shops and houses threw out their Georgian windows and doors and encroached upon the highway so that when John was visiting, or Mary shopping, it meant constantly mounting steps or dodging porches. It was not long before John fell prey to the uneven streets of London. In April of the year of his arrival the rector was standing at his own front door; he stepped back carelessly, tripped over a large stone and was thrown over a short post. Nursing a bruised and dislocated shoulder John remarked to Mary that in all his travels and dangers, it was the only serious accident he could remember! In the middle of the street ran the open sewer, a gutter, which was generally blocked and consequently foul. A cart or carriage passing through this at an inopportune moment was disastrous for Mary's clean white dress and John's neatly brushed shoes. There was no law of the road and only the most adept survived!

Lighting was poor and patchy. Gas would not be on the streets for another thirty years, and since the lamp-lighters frequently sold a proportion of their oil, few streets had any light at all after midnight.

When John negotiated the city in the course of his pastoral duties, he would have little difficulty appreciating why Napoleon later referred to England as a nation of small shopkeepers. Everywhere the retailer threw open his doors to invite the customer, and Mary Newton was offered everything she could ever need, if only she could afford it. The street sellers were at their noisiest. The apple woman, the bandbox man, the bellows mender, the bed-mat man, and the rabbit seller, all added their cries to the scores of others proffering everything from brick dust (for sharpening knives) to muffins.

The noise in a London Street was almost unbearable for the quiet country curate accustomed, for the past sixteen years at least, to the lapping of a meandering river, the song of the birds and the cows tearing softly at the grass. In London the women gossiped at their doors, children screamed, cart men cursed their animals and each other, street sellers yelled out their wares and out-yelled their competitors, horses kicked and pranced, men fought and crowds gathered; the city of London groaned under a babel of confused shouting.

FILTH

The Fleet River meandered through the green fields of Islington and nodded beside the small-pox hospital as a prophecy of its later course. It passed under four bridges at Bridewell, Fleet Street, Fleet Lane and Holborn, which area, a contemporary claimed, was « heaped with filth and ruins and the hiding-places of a numerous swarm of the most flagitious of our poor ». The Fleet River passed through the city as a vast, slow-moving canal of filth, changed its name from river to « ditch » and spewed its vile load into the Thames at Blackfriars. There were no sewers, and all imaginable and unimaginable rubbish and excrement were tipped onto the streets in the hope that the rain would wash it away. Occasionally it did, but the stench on a warm summer afternoon was unbearable.

The coal fires puffed their clouds of choking sulphur into the sky and formed a protective blanket above the city, designed to keep fresh air and sunlight out and the smell of sewage and dirt in. John coughed his way into the alleys and homes and longed for the fragrant meadow-sweet that carpeted the fields beside Olney Church, and the delicate honeysuckle that twined around the hedgerows and gardens of his old country parish.

The slums of Newton's London had to be visited to be believed; and Newton did visit them. Overcrowding was only one of the many evils, and it is not hard to imagine the results of sleeping seventeen people in one room. One of the most notorious slum areas was Locks Field, just off the fashionable New Kent Road. Barefoot, unwashed children roamed the streets, children of « whores, pick-pockets, footpads, housebreakers, and thieves of every description »; a piece of dirty pudding and brown greasy potatoes

The slums of Newton's London.

were their meal for the day. The men lolled, dirty and dishevelled; the women, mostly common property of the men, appeared at the door in their greasy, torn garments, with matted hair dropping to the broken stays of their bodice, and threw the day's garbage into the street.

John was more familiar with the ground nearer the river. If the Billingsgate fisherwomen were coarse, loud and quarrelsome, it was the women of the riverside taverns who were most wretched; they owned nothing, lived nowhere, and by the age of twenty-five usually journeyed, unmourned, to the great churchyard of St. George's, Ratcliffe.

Lord Vice owned the slums, and Filth and Lice were tenants. Drink dried up tears and burned up hearts so that thousands seemed to live and die without a soul. London's only answer to the slum dwellers was to hang sufficient numbers at each session « to maintain a balance ».

VIOLENCE

It was the age of « do it yourself justice » and even Dr Johnson walked the city with a stout stick which he dexterously used upon pick-pockets and louts. Back in 1752 Sir Horace Mann complained: « One is forced to travel, even at noon, as if one were going to battle », and it had not changed at all by the time John Newton arrived. Fine ladies were still escorted to and from their card parties by boys with clubs.

John had to learn a new vocabulary that described the felons of London: buffers, smashers, noses, sharpers, bustlers—the list was endless. Robbery invaded every corner of city life; the crowd was infested with pick-pockets, just as almost everyone's hair was infested with lice, and the stage coach rarely delivered all its packages. The servants of the rich, the gardeners, the vendors, everyone was « in it » together. Fortunately, John had learnt to recognise the twister and thief by his long experience at sea. The highwayman commanded the heaths and moors (it was the romantic age of the legends of Dick Turpin and Tom King) and the footpad commanded the streets of the city. No-one went abroad at night unless he was a fool or well-armed with pistol and sword.

The prisons bred savage criminals. Men and women were crowded into filthy and cold rooms and the conditions here were excelled in misery only on the ships of war. There was nothing for prisoners to do in gaol except to perfect the vices which had brought them there, and succumb to the choking « gaol fever ».

When John and Mary arrived in London the dreadful march from Newgate prison to the Tyburn still persisted, at least until 1784. Two years before John and Mary arrived, Wesley had buried honest Silas Told. This tall, lean, ex-sailor had devoted many years to the prisons. He preached to the inmates of every London prison and climbed into those deathly carts as they drew away to Tyburn; he led many to a faith in Christ. John Newton doubtless knew of him, but Silas Told would no longer ride in the cart as a messenger from heaven, and as John surveyed the grisly spectacle of a Tyburn day he determined that he would follow old Silas into the prisons.

The day on which Newgate disgorged its cartloads of prisoners to be hanged near the turnpike at the end of Oxford Street, was always a festival day. The journey lasted half an hour and the road was as thronged as it would be for a coronation. Stalls for gin and geneva, stalls for nuts and gingerbread, players and clowns all supplied and entertained the crowd. The cartloads of condemned consisted of the defiant smiling highwayman, nonchalant as he rode ceremoniously to his death, the poor gibbering fool who died because no-one cared to plead his cause, the husband who dared to return from his sentence of life transportation, the father who stole above one shilling to silence the cries of his starving family, and the miserable girl who clung to her baby for those last precious minutes before it was snatched from her arms as the noose fell round her neck. Life was cheap, easy to hire and easily dispensable. The public gallows was never wanting for clients. At whatever point the visitor entered London there were gibbets. Along the banks of the Thames, in Fleet Street, the Strand, Covent Garden and of course, at the end of Oxford Street. « Cross any of the heaths, commons or forests near London », it was claimed, « and you would be startled by the creaking of the chains from which some gibbetted highwayman was dropping piecemeal ». The heart of London was cruel and hard. To this city John Newton came as a minister of the Gospel.

EXTRAVAGANCE

The other face of eighteenth century London was extravagant, luxurious, but just as decadent, and its peace and happiness was just as illusive. The rich lived on the outskirts of the city, bathing in the luxury of their excessive fortunes. Their large houses and extensive gardens, and the small army of servants,

The other face of London.

spoke eloquently of a society as wasteful as it was powerful. Nearer the city the middle-class merchants set up their comfortable homes and rode into town each day to conduct their business.

One part of London worked fourteen hours a day,

six days a week, in the stagnant filth and choking dust-laden air of the back streets, to be rewarded with eight to fifteen shillings a week. Another part of the city brawled and stole, for these had no work. But the rest played cards, drank tea and coffee, visited exclusive clubs, where they smoked and gambled, attended the theatre and flirted; all this for seven days a week on a fortune of anything from sixty thousand to half a million pounds.

It was the age of the flowered, tight-fitting waist-coat, the white silk coat, the gold-laced hat, the ruffles and dainty neck tie, the sword and sword sash, the powdered wig, the clean shaven face, the white silk stockings and gold buckled shoes. Complete with cane and snuff-box the young gentleman was ready for the day's pleasure.

The lady matched her man in splendour, and at church she would distract the men with her beauty and the women with her dress. Her cream skirts trimmed with Olney lace, the light blue shoulder knots, the amber necklace, brown Swedish gloves and silver bracelet, a large-flowered silk belt of green and grey and yellow with its bow at the side. That monstrous hooped dress, minute waist and enormous hair set, a hideous three feet high occasionally, were also becoming the vogue.

The main employment of the idle rich was gambling. In the exclusive clubs the men lost and won fortunes at a sitting. Lord Carlisle once lost ten thousand pounds at one cast of the hazard. The ladies played cards at home from lunchtime to bedtime and the Government joined in with a state lottery which, in the year Newton preached his first sermon at St. Mary's, sold forty nine thousand tickets and distributed four hundred and ninety thousand pounds in prize money.

ST. MARY WOOLNOTH

When John accepted the invitation to become rector at the united parishes of St. Mary Woolnoth with St. Mary Woolchurch, there were just over one hundred and fifty houses in his parish and his annual stipend amounted to approximately one pound for each home. The heavy, plain building with its « pretty organ » (most of the London parishes had no organ), was situated in Lombard Street, close by the Bank of England, the Stock Market, and the General Post Office. The Post Office came to Lombard Street in 1690 and remained there until 1829; it was providentially situated for the man whose letters travelled throughout the kingdom. From here John could arrange for a letter to be delivered in London for one penny (the charge had not risen for one hundred years!), in Edinburgh for seven-pence or in America for one shilling.

The simplicity of life in Olney became a confused whirl of noise and movement in London. In Olney the few who were rich managed the many who were poor with a condescending benevolence, but here everyone jostled and fought to possess anything and continued to jostle and fight to keep it.

The heavy plain building in Lombard Street.

Newton was a practical, down-to-earth man, with little time or patience for the frills and frivolity of the rich. He was not one to seek society and the wealthy parishioners soon realised this. They simply ignored him. John wrote sadly to Thomas Scott on May 29th: « At St. Mary Woolnoth I seem to do just what I please, my parishioners give me no trouble, some of them attend. But I have not received one invitation into their houses, except from the few who are serious. The few times I have been sent for to christen etc. they behave extremely polite, I have a hope of being better acquainted in time but Rome was not built in a day ». The patient rector was prepared to wait his time; he was determined that the slum dweller, merchant and aristocrat would all hear the Gospel sooner or later. But John often found it hard to bring these people to a proper conversation and he bared his problem and fears to Scott as he continued: « How to force myself upon them I know not. To be received as a guest by the rich people, except I could be received as a minister, would not answer my end, and to go down upon their ground in hopes of inducing them to come up to mine, would be rather a hazardous experiment. I dare not venture upon it... » As John was afraid to offend, so he was afraid to compromise.

The spiritual life of London was at a low ebb; certainly the preaching of Whitefield had changed many, but this great man's lips had been silenced by death ten years before; John and Charles Wesley were now old men. When John Newton came to London, he and Mr Romaine at St. Anne's Blackfriars were the only two evangelical Church of England ministers in the city.

TMD 14

PULPIT AND GALLERY

Like Olney, St. Mary's had no gallery when John Newton arrived but, like Olney, one was soon built. It was not long before this fervent evangelical attracted an ever growing congregation. In an age when everyone kept a diary, wrote letters and wanted to read the diary and letters of everyone else, John Newton's correspondence had particular value. His *Authentic Narrative* and *Omicron* were reaching a wider and wider public and had already been translated into Dutch; during his first year in London John published *Cardiphonia,* a title chosen by Cowper, being one hundred and fifty one warm and personal letters; they were « utterances of the heart ».

It says much for Newton's wide and impartial care that the first twenty-six letters were addressed to Lord Dartmouth (though names were not affixed to the published letters) and seven more were written to Newton's own maid, Sally Johnson. They were warm, pastoral letters and he confided to Sally: « You are often in my thoughts, and seldom omitted in my prayers ». A letter written in 1769 reveals not only his concern for Sally to find a satisfying faith in Christ, which she did, but also his concern for her sister who was very ill. Soon visitors and residents travelled to Lombard Street to hear the author of these valuable letters. They thronged into the building and became « a numerous and attentive congregation ».

The church filled with the shopkeepers, merchants and financiers who then complained that their seats were being taken by others. A church warden suggested that Mr Newton should preach away on occasions and without notice so that if the congregation could never be sure of his presence, the number of visitors might be reduced! John smiled and promised to do something. A gallery was built.

His preaching, though no more graceful than it was at Olney, was just as powerful. The old slave in Africa, who had once tied his hook to a piece of string and baited the fish with the gut of a hen, believed that the fisherman's best fishing time was not when he held the neatest rods, hooks or lines, or when he ventured out in the most favourable weather, but when he had the greatest catch of fish!

This practical, down-to-earth approach meant that no-one was spared the application of his message. One Sunday the rector climbed into his ornately carved pulpit with its large, spreading sounding board and informed his congregation that a bill (notice) had appeared in the vestibule of St. Mary's to the effect that a young man, having come into the possession of a considerable fortune, desired the prayers of the congregation that he might be preserved from the snares to which it exposed him. « Now », responded the pastor, « if the man had lost a fortune, the world would not have wondered to have seen him put up a bill, but this man has been better taught. »

The busy life which Newton led did not always allow him adequate time for sermon preparation and there were Sunday mornings when he had nothing in mind for his people. « Lord, I am empty indeed », he often exclaimed, but found comfort in trusting God to

211

fill his mouth when legitimate business had stolen the hours needed for preparation. In 1784 John found little difficulty in gaining material for a series of sermons. There was a Handel Commemoration in Westminster Abbey, and Newton, with all his aversion to Handel's use of Scripture as « the subject of a musical entertainment » preached fifty messages from the great composer's « Messiah ».

Newton continued to preach, as he had always done, not for dissension, but for disseminating the truth. He aimed to lead his hearers to a growing and more experimental knowledge of the Son of God and a life of faith in Him. Consequently he avoided issues that he knew would inflame, and in his enlarged sphere of service « churchmen and dissenters, Calvinists and Arminians, Methodists and Moravians, now and then, I believe, Papists and Quakers, sit quietly to hear me... ». However it must not be imagined that Newton therefore sat loosely to his doctrine. In writing to an enquirer in one of his *Omicron* letters, John dealt freely with the « Doctrines of Election and Final Perseverance ». He was quite sure that, not by « noisy disputation », but by « humble waiting upon God in prayer, and a careful perusal of his holy Word » his correspondent would soon view Calvin's doctrines in a favourable light; John then set out to explain, from Scripture, the total depravity of human nature, and the need for God's undeserved grace to change it. He believed equally in the Christian's perseverance, certain that the salvation gained for us by Christ could never be lost by ourselves. The more we realised « our inability from first to last, the more excellent will Jesus appear ». Elsewhere John preferred the term invincible grace, rather than irresistible grace; his own experience had taught him that God's grace can often be resisted by the sinner but if God has once set His love upon a man he can never persist for long in his stubbornness. Newton concluded without fear of contradiction, « that the doctrines of grace are doctrines according to godliness ». And John Newton's letters reflected his pulpit.

The issue was once more easily settled by an old lady in Olney who remarked to Newton: « Ah, I have long settled that point: for, if God had not chosen me before I was born, I am sure he would have seen nothing in me to have chosen me for afterwards ».

The uncompromising stand of Newton on the evangelical faith would never allow him to become entangled in disputes over details, and in a day when duels were fought over the definition of a word this spirit was urgently needed. A group of ministers was once disputing whether faith or repentance was first in order. Newton listened intently for a while and then added his own point: « Gentlemen, are not the heart and lungs of a man both equally necessary to the life of the man? » « Yes surely », his friends replied. « Well, tell me », continued Newton, « which of these began to play first? This resembles the point you have been discussing ». Likewise he dealt with another issue. « Many have puzzled themselves about the origins of evil », he commented. « I observe that there is evil, and that there is a way to escape it, and with this I begin and end ». In 1784 he wrote his *Apologia* which was a series of four letters to an Independent minister setting out his own reasons for remaining within the Established Church.

THE HOME AT HOXTON

Mary settled down with maid Sally to make the new home as comfortable as possible. It was not long before the same trail of visitors, that she had become accustomed to at Olney, commenced here also. Now her husband was more accessible and in between his duties, running about to look on other people, he found himself sitting at home « like a tame elephant or a monkey for other people to come look at me ». Mary worked in her little garden and asked John, when next he wrote to Cowper, to request some « curious seeds », William would know what she meant. John obeyed and said his wife was asking for what she called « curious seeds », adding in bewilderment, « as if there were some seeds that are not curious ».

Betsy Catlett was away for most of the time at a boarding school in Highgate, and her place was fleetingly filled by Eliza Cunningham. Mary's sister, Elizabeth, had married and moved to Scotland where her eldest son died after an injury to his leg. Susie, the next in line, developed consumption (tuberculosis) and Elizabeth took the child to Edinburgh for treatment. Whilst she was there her husband died and his death was followed post haste by Susie's. The remaining child, Eliza, was welcomed into the Newton's home, and shortly after her arrival her mother, who had remained in Scotland too weak to leave, died of consumption also. Consumption carried off a large proportion of the population, and it was hardly surprising since milk straight from the udder, the best breeding ground for the bacillus, was a great delicacy.   But there was nothing unusually tragic in this sad picture.   In 1770, of every one thousand children born in London, and seventeen thousand were, five hundred and fifty three were dead before the age of five and the clergy attended more funerals than christenings in that year.   Exactly half the coffins ordered were small ones.   One of Newton's most promising curates died young in October 1796 but not before he had been bereaved of his wife and four small children.   The Cunninghams were fortunate to have lived as long as they had!

Elizabeth Cunningham came into the home as a healthy fourteen year old girl and the Newtons rejoiced in their two young nieces.   It was not long, however, before Eliza showed symptoms of the same wasting disease; she could rarely go out, but sat and read, or sewed, or played her harpsichord.   John and Mary looked upon their « heap of untold gold » and waited for the end.   Eliza was unafraid to die, she rested in her uncle's certain faith and settled the text he was to preach at her funeral, and the « Olney Hymn » that should be sung.

After her death John published a little pamphlet entitled, *A Monument to the Praise of the Lord's Goodness and to the Memory of dear Eliza Cunningham*.   It was dated from Hoxton October 13th, 1785, circulated privately, and concluded: « I shall be glad if this little narrative may prove an encouragement to my friends who have children ».   Cowper thought it was « just what it should be ».

After a brief separation, when Mary took Eliza to Southampton in August 1785 in the vain hope of a recovery, John and Mary were never again separated until the sad year of 1790. Each year the rector and his wife toured the country, as they had done at Olney, and refreshed themselves in the clean air of the English countryside. They even went to the sea at Brighton where the ugly bathing machines were marshalled on the beach waiting to swallow the lady and give her a modest dip. Mrs Newton was enjoying better health than for many a long day and John's love for her, after thirty five years of married life, was undiminished.

A PASTOR'S STUDY

John preferred to walk to church when possible; it gave him time to observe and think. But he was saddened to see many merchants still at their trades and the barbers' prentices hurrying from home to home with the Sunday wigs prepared for church. However, the people were beginning to listen, lives were changing and doors were opening to the new rector.

Men and women moved in and out of the study and vestry; letters arrived and were answered. Newton was in great demand. A party of dissenters urged him to set down an outline of a system of study to be adopted by a dissenting academy shortly to be opened under William Bull at Newport Pagnell. John agreed, though wondered what their excuse would be for applying to a Churchman for counsel! He wrote a preface for a new volume of poems by Cowper: a preface that delighted the poet but so troubled the publisher by its religious language that he requested that it should be withdrawn. Letters poured in and out, and the correspondence, that so nibbled away his time at Olney, swallowed even larger amounts here in London. Almost every post informed Newton that his published sermons, letters and the *Authentic Narrative* were proving of immense value in the country, across the borders in Scotland, on the Continent of Europe and in America also. Invitations to preach came from far afield and the steady flow of visitors continued. His time was divided between preaching, writing and counselling. Time passed quickly, and the diary of one day could be the diary of a year.

The care and wisdom of the preacher at St. Mary's attracted many people into his vestry. But not all received the advice they came for. The lady, who came to be congratulated because she had received a prize with her lottery ticket, was sent away with the assurance: « Madam, as for a friend under temptation, I will pray for you ». During his years as a seaman and even once whilst in Liverpool, John had purchased lottery tickets and had commended the outcome to God! But he knew better now. A group of merchants were warned: « There is a great and old established house, which does much business and causes no small disturbance in the world and in the church. The firm is Satan, Self and Co. ». Members of the Protestant Association urged him to be more specific in his denunciation of the Papacy; Newton, who hated the system of Rome as much as the Association, replied with a twinkle: « I have read of many wicked popes, but the worst pope I ever met with is Pope Self ». Even to the spiritual request for a prayer circle to be formed on a Sunday evening, the rector responded with enthusiasm but added: « When I have been preaching and nine p.m. comes round I find myself more disposed for supper and bed than prayer ». But many came in deep spiritual need, and such enquirers at the study door found nothing but care and wise counsel.

FROM COLEMAN STREET TO INDIA

Claudius Buchanan was one of the first Englishmen to care sufficiently for the spiritual plight of the people of India to spend his life in their service. During his service as vice-provost of the college at Fort William, he laboured with tireless energy to promote education among the natives and lead them from their superstitions. He toured the country, translated the New Testament into a local dialect, and supported, at his own expense, an Armenian Christian who was translating the Scriptures into Chinese. He died in 1815 whilst revising a Syriac translation of the New Testament. For his outstanding service to India he was awarded an honorary doctorate from Glasgow and Cambridge. But his spiritual life began with an unsigned letter to the rector of St. Mary's.

Buchanan was born in 1766 at Cambuslang near Glasgow, but though he grew up at the scene of some of Whitefield's most powerful preaching twenty-four years earlier, he threw off any childhood religion and set out for London at the age of twenty-one earning his passage with his violin as an eighteenth century busker. In London he lived in obscure lodgings and sold his clothes and books to buy food. For three tedious years he lived « I knew not how, in a state of forgetfulness or mental intoxication... ». He led a very dissipated, irreligious life and never thought of any religious duty. A friend introduced Buchanan to Doddridge's *Rise and Progress of Religion in the Soul* and a few other good books. He was not much affected but a letter from his mother urged him to join « the crowded audience at a church in Lombard Street ». Subsequently Claudius wrote to the Rev John Newton and confessed: « When you spoke I thought I heard the words of eternal life; I listened with avidity, and wished that you had preached till midnight ».

The following Sunday Newton gave out a notice in church that if the person who had sent him a letter without signature or address would care to contact him, he would gladly discuss matters further. Buchanan came to the pastor's new home at 6, Coleman Street Buildings « and experienced such a happy hour as I ought not to forget. If he had been my father, he could not have expressed more solicitude for my welfare ». Buchanan read *An Authentic Narrative,* as did all who called on the old captain, breakfasted often with the Newtons and, with new life in Christ, was sent by John Thornton to Cambridge. In 1794 Newton first urged Buchanan to consider service in India.

This sound advice to Buchanan was perhaps influenced by a visit Newton received a year earlier from the Northamptonshire cobbler, William Carey. Carey had long prepared himself for service in India and by March 1793 he was ready to leave. Faced with a most harassing week, unable to obtain the necessary permits for his entry to India as a missionary, Carey called on « good old father Newton ». The baptist missionary asked Newton's counsel in the event of the East India Company sending Carey and his companion Thomas straight home on their arrival in Bengal. The old rector replied gravely: « Conclude that your Lord has nothing there for you to accomplish. If He have, no power on earth can prevent you ». The two men corresponded frequently and Newton's influence was at times a much needed help when Carey was snubbed by Churchmen in India. Newton's love for the servants of God, whatever their denomination, is well illustrated by his commendation later: « Such a man as Carey is more to me than bishop or archbishop: he is an apostle. »

It was while John and Mary were still living at Hoxton that two other people entered their home, each preceded by a letter. William Wilberforce and Hannah More had been thrown into the whirl of London society, but it was the wisdom of the old sailor that led them into lives of satisfaction and usefulness.

CHAPTER 10.

WILBERFORCE
AND HANNAH MORE

IF BILLY TURNS METHODIST

On Sunday, December 4th, 1785, an elegant and cultured young man stepped into the porch of St. Mary Woolnoth and delivered a note into the hand of « old Newton at his church ».   The text of that letter was both mysterious in its content and far reaching in its effects:

« Sir,
There is no need of apology for intruding on you, when the errand is religion.   I wish to have some serious conversation with you, and will take the liberty of calling on you for that purpose, in half an hour; when, if you cannot receive me, you will have the goodness to let me have a letter put into my hands at the door, naming a time and place for our meeting, the earlier the more agreeable to me.   I have had ten thousand doubts within myself, whether or not I should discover myself to you; but every argument against doing it has its foundation in pride.   I am sure you will hold yourself bound to let no-one living know of this application, or of my visit, till I release you from the obligation.

P.S.   Remember that I must be secret, and that the gallery of the House is now so universally attended, that the face of a member of Parliament is pretty well known. »

Old Newton could not admit the troubled enquirer at once but arranged to see him the following Wednesday.   At the appointed hour, the correspondent arrived in Hoxton Square but found his courage failing; if society knew that he was about to converse with the evangelical, methodistical preacher; if society guessed the turbulent state of his mind and the serious purpose of his visit, then the whole of his political future could be ruined!   After walking about the Square once or twice and persuading himself that the issues were too vital to set aside for the fear of man, the Member of Parliament for Hull and Yorkshire was ushered into the study of the Rector of St. Mary's.

FROM HULL TO WIMBLEDON

William Wilberforce was born in Hull on August 24th, 1759. He was educated at Hull Grammar School until the untimely death of his father when, at the age of nine, he was sent to London where an uncle possessed a charming house in the heart of the picturesque beauty of the Wimbledon countryside. This family was deeply affected by Methodist principles; George Whitefield frequently visited the home and the curate of Olney became a regular preacher there also.   When news of this state of affairs reached the Wilberforce home in Yorkshire, there was great alarm; the paternal grandfather declared: « If Billy turns Methodist he shall not have a sixpence of mine, » and Billy was at once recalled to Hull. As a matter of fact the evangelical influence of his uncle's home left only a faint impression upon Billy's mind and after completing his education at St. John's College, Cambridge, he stood as a Member for Hull in the election of 1780 and at the age of twenty one years entered the House of Commons where he continued to serve for the next forty five years.

Entering Parliament meant that Wilberforce entered a fashionable society, and his considerable fortune enabled him to enjoy extravagance and fast living. A personable young man, Wilberforce loved the parties and enjoyed music. His voice possessed a quality that earned the commendation of the Prince Regent who claimed he would come at any time to hear Wilberforce sing.

When the home at Wimbledon was left him in his uncle's will, Wilberforce fled to this country refuge and in 1784 became Member of Parliament for Yorkshire. During the autumn Wilberforce visited the Continent for an extended holiday with his mother and sister, and took with him as a companion his old school master, Isaac Milner, brother of the church historian Joseph. Though himself a brilliant scholar, Milner was a rough Yorkshireman complete with broad accent and a rugged, but firm, Methodism. Wilberforce at least knew how to be serious about religion and was a loyal Churchman. Back in 1782 he wrote triumphantly in his diary one Sunday of a success with the young Chancellor of the Exchequer:

« Persuaded Pitt to Church ». It was not long before
Milner and Wilberforce were engaged in long and deep
conversations about evangelical truth.

In 1785 Wilberforce returned to the whirl of London
society and he threw himself into the balls and
concerts, the operas and theatres, the Sunday dinners,
exclusive clubs and the gaming tables. Yet for all his
fortune, he gambled little and drank less. In the
summer he returned to the Continent with Milner and
together they read from Doddridge's *Rise and Progress
of Religion in the Soul.* By the time he returned to
England there was an evident change in his mind but
not such that he would call conversion. He recorded
sadly in his journal: « I must awake to my dangerous
state, and never be at rest 'till I have made my peace
with God. My heart is so hard, my blindness so
great, that I cannot get a due hatred of sin, though I
see I am all corrupt, and blinded to the perception of
spiritual things. »

OLD NEWTON

Milner persuaded his young companion to visit
Newton, and so, on December 7th, 1785, the venerable
saint and the young M.P. talked together. When
Wilberforce came away he found his mind that evening in a sad state; he could scarcely pray, but determined to hope and wait on God. The following
Sunday, Wilberforce was a member of the congregation at St. Mary's. He gazed around at the large,
well-packed congregation, the new wooden gallery

running round the walls, that grotesque pulpit and the even more grotesque Corinthian pillars, twelve of them. The poor, the merchants, the rich were all there: the ladies with their crinkling, rustling dresses and the men starched and stiff. But the minister dispelled attention to the world, and when William left St. Mary's that Sunday he recorded in his journal: « Heard Newton on the addiction of the soul to God—Excellent. He shows his whole heart is engaged. » Two days later he was reading, with great profit, Newton's *Authentic Narrative*.

During the next few months Wilberforce resorted frequently to Lombard Street and Charles Square and his diary and letters were filled with unashamed references to Newton: « Went to Newton's, but when he prayed I was cold and dead; and the moment we were out of his house, seriousness decayed ». « Colder than ever—very unhappy—called at Newton's, and bitterly moved; he comforted me. » On December 20th he recorded: « Newton's Church... not quite so warm (presumably a reference to his own soul!) but still a good hope—I trust God is with me... I stayed in town to attend the ordinances, and have been gloriously blessed in them. »

By mid-January 1786 Wilberforce had found a joyous and decided Christian faith and expressed his gratitude to Newton. He resolved, by Newton's advice, to remain in politics and bring his Christian influence to bear in this realm; that decision was momentous. William no longer wished to remain incognito and he released the rector from his obligation of secrecy. On January 12th he wrote : « Expect

225

to hear myself now universally given out to be a methodist; may God grant it may be said with truth ».   Billy had inherited grandfather's fortune *and* had become a Methodist!

The relationship of Newton and Wilberforce continued unbroken through succeeding years.   In 1792 the minister was asking the Member of Parliament for advice on whether or not he should patronise West Indian sugar, and in 1795 Newton wrote commending *Practical Christianity*, a little book that Wilberforce had published with great success; Newton had read it three times « with increasing satisfaction ».   John wrote at least three times a year and by 1804 the experienced politician was writing in the most tender and affectionate terms to the venerable warrior of the cross.

AN EVANGELICAL POLITICIAN

The humanity and reforms of Wilberforce were a direct result, as were those of Shaftesbury a century later, of his firm evangelical faith.   After a life of bringing children up from the mines and out from the factories, down from chimneys and away from the slums, Shaftesbury declared to his biographer : « I think a man's religion, if it is worth anything, should enter into every sphere of life, and rule his conduct in every relation.   I have always been—and, please God, always shall be—an Evangelical of the Evangelicals, and no biography can represent me that does not fully and emphatically represent my religious views. »   The same may rightly be said of Wilberforce.

When the change in Wilberforce became known, his family were deeply concerned and his close friend, William Pitt, by now the twenty four year old Prime Minister, concluded that he must be unwell. No longer were the courtesies of Society pleasant to him, and he remarked of one who had flattered him to the point of servility: « I had rather he had spit in my face ». But Wilberforce loved life and threw himself into it with untiring zeal. Lord Macaulay, the brilliant historian of Victoria's reign, remarked at the death of Wilberforce, that this desire to live he found strange in a man with so firm a belief in a future world and with « an impaired fortune, a weak spine, and a worn out stomach ». But perhaps Macaulay had never learnt that, contrary to popular opinion, those who are most heavenly minded are also of most earthly use.

With his strong « methodistical views » Wilberforce remained a strong Churchman, and as the years passed he became more suspicious of some over-enthusiastic Methodists and was glad to move from Wimbledon lest he should become « a bigoted despised Methodist ». Similarly, he suspected dissent, concluding that it was « highly injurious to the interests of religion in the long run ». However, his evangelical spirit embraced all who loved Christ and proclaimed the truth. In 1798 he vigorously defended the Jersey Methodists who refused Sunday drill in His Majesty's Army, and Wilberforce, urged by his old counsellor at St. Mary's, was a strong supporter of the Toleration Act. He could number among his friends many of these dissenters and despised Methodists, even if not the bigotted ones.

In politics Wilberforce was independent, unfettered and fearless. In the various issues in which he joined battle, his loyalty to principle brought down upon him, at various times, the wrath of Pitt, politicians and ministers of all shades; the royal family and even King George himself found cause to oppose him. Once the populace mobbed him for his unpopular views and he was given police protection. As a speaker he had no equal in the House, not even Pitt excepted, and this « nightingale of the House of Commons » possessed a brilliant wit, a quick and alert mind, a thorough understanding of the mood of the House and could hold the members enthralled throughout a three hour speech.

THE ABOLITION OF SLAVERY

Slavery was the great issue for which the name of Wilberforce is for ever remembered. For years the Quakers had tried to force the slavery issue upon the nation's conscience and, in 1774, even John Wesley added his power to the debate in *Thoughts on Slavery*. Two years later a resolution before Parliament « that the slave trade was contrary to the laws of God and the rights of man » gained little support. In 1787 the *Society for the Abolition of the Slave Trade* was formed with Granville Sharp as chairman. The same year Wilberforce undertook to be parliamentary spokesman and the spearhead of the anti-slavery movement. With John Newton as his counsellor and confidant he had little fear of confusing his facts.

In spite of an immediate breakdown in his health, at which time the doctors gave him only three weeks to live, Wilberforce was back in action by the end of the year confirming his involvement in the issue by noting in his diary: « Slave business all the evening, with only biscuit and wine and water ».   He spent eight or nine hours a day on the slave business, and the terrible stories he encountered during the day gave him frightful dreams of slavery at night.

On May 11th, 1789, amidst mounting opposition from the powerful and wealthy West Indian merchants and their incessant wailing of economic ruin to the colonies and England, Wilberforce opened the debate in the House of Commons with a masterful three and a half hour speech.   Forty-four years later, and just six days before his death on July 29th, 1833, a Bill for the emancipation of all slaves was carried through Parliament and his life's work was over.

The French Revolution settled any hopes of an early success for the abolitionists.   The Government panicked at the thought of any liberty, anywhere, that might lead to a British Bastille.   But Wilberforce pressed on.   By the beginning of 1790 Wilberforce was chairman of a select committee and much of his time was spent calling witnesses and filing the ever mounting documents and testimonies.   The Privy Council was also busy with the issue and when John Newton was called to testify before it, the Prime Minister personally conducted the old slave captain to his seat and introduced him as the friend of Mr Wilberforce.

Wilberforce opened the debate in the house.

There can be no doubt that the conscience and energy of Newton was a great inspiration to Wilberforce. In 1787 he had published *Thoughts on the African Slave Trade* and this became one of the most powerful weapons in the abolitionists' armoury. Wilberforce circulated thousands of copies throughout the kingdom. The pamphlet was well reasoned and with a strong appeal to the heart. The old captain had his journal for the years 1750-54 beside him as he wrote, and although « what I did I did ignorantly, » he now set the whole of his considerable weight and power behind the attempts to abolish the terrible traffic.

The first argument of these *Thoughts* was the appalling loss of life to British seamen engaged in the trade and he estimated that one in five never returned. Secondly, he wrote, the bestial trade corrupted « every gentle and humane disposition » in man and made our sailors little better than brute beasts. It was wise to begin here; few in England cared for the slaves, but a few more cared for the sailors. But Newton went on to detail the torture, cruelty and barbarity to which the slaves were exposed; he dispensed with the suggestion that they were only unfeeling animals, claiming that he had met with more instances of humanity and honesty among the negroes than among most of the white men employed in the trade. He described the horror of the Middle Passage and graphically bore testimony to the ill-treatment they received in the West Indies where it was established to be cheaper to work a slave to death and then replace him than to treat him well and allow him a longer life. Slaves rarely lived above nine years in these conditions.

This was strong and telling material. Yet eloquence, reason and humanity were defeated by stupid prejudice and vested interests and for many years the « pigmies », as the abolitionists were called, made little progress against the « giants ». In 1788, the Corporation of Liverpool, from which city Newton had sailed as a slave trader and in which he had served as an Excise Officer, petitioned Parliament against the abolition proposals « which so essentially concern the welfare of the Town and Port of Liverpool ». In spite of the unceasing labour, and over five hundred petitions around the country, Pitt lost interest in the cause, the royal family declared itself firmly against abolition, and a Bill for « Gradual Abolition » settled the issue into a small corner until the nineteenth century.

Wilberforce, encouraged by Newton, brought in a motion each year, until by 1798 it was lost by only four votes. Yet by the turn of the century the trade had actually doubled and William felt sickened by public life and public men. In 1804 the Commons returned a majority of 124 to 49 in favour, but the Lords spiritual and temporal, blocked the Bill after its second reading. Pitt died in 1806 and the new Government agreed to take up the cause. General abolition received the royal assent on February 23rd, 1807, with two days to spare, for on February 25th the Government collapsed. Not until 1833 were all British owned slaves finally set free.

Thus, the efforts of this man in Parliament, a band of faithful and diligent workers, reams of pamphlets and a wise and repentant slave captain achieved for Britain in 1833 what the deaths of nearly half a million men and one of the bloodiest civil wars in history accomplished for America in 1865. The slaves were free.

THE CLAPHAM GROUP

Wilberforce should never be remembered for the abolition movement alone. He joined with a number of other young evangelical Churchmen to form the « Clapham Group »; their aim was to bring true spiritual life back into the Church of England and to help humanity wherever they could. Henry, the son of John Thornton, was a member, and a close friend of Wilberforce. They established a colony for freed slaves in Sierra Leone, financed the West Country village schools started by Hannah More, and formed the *Society for the Reformation of Manners*, which in spite of its curious title achieved valuable reforms against the blasphemy, indecent literature, unlicensed amusements and excessive punishments of the day. Wilberforce visited the condemned in Newgate and supported Elizabeth Fry in her valuable work. In 1796 he took up the many abuses in London hospitals and worked at them until someone did something. In 1800 Wilberforce, with the strong encouragement of Newton, helped to establish the Church Missionary Society, first discussed in John's Eclectic Society, and by his labours many missionaries were sent abroad; the name of Wilberforce is found as a Sponsor of the Bible Society in 1808.

The Clapham evangelicals were tireless. When the

Bill for abolition passed by 283 votes to 16, Wilberforce crossed to his house in Palace Yard and was met by a crowd of well-wishers. Henry Thornton, also a member of Parliament, was there. « Well Henry », he asked, « what shall we abolish next? » Thornton linked his arms and walked with him to the door. « The lottery, I think », he replied.

Wilberforce married in 1797 and was devoted to his wife and family. He put « first, my children; secondly Parliament, » yet gave his life to the cause of Christian humanity. In large measure it was all due to that first, faltering encounter with John Newton, and the subsequent advice and counsel that could always be obtained from the old Rector at St. Mary's.

HANNAH'S DELUSIVE HOPE

In 1773, a slender, graceful and altogether pretty young lady of 28 years made her first visit to London. She was immediately welcomed into the circle of privileged friendship with the great Dr Johnson and at once became the centre of attraction, admiration and the flattery at which Johnson and his friends excelled. Hannah More had published her first play, *The Search after Happiness*, in that year, and it was an instant success. Ironically the title was to prove a description of the next few years of her life.

By 1777 Hannah produced two ballads and these, together with a play entitled *Percy*, a tragedy in five acts, which was first performed on December 10th, ensured her fame and from then on everything she wrote became a best seller.   *Percy* ran for twenty-two nights, spectacular in those days, and continued on and off until 1815.   The success of this play alone earned the maiden lady from Gloucester a name engraved into the history of the English theatre, nearly six hundred pounds, and a nervous breakdown.

A FRIEND OF GARRICK

In the year John Newton was put on board the *Pegasus,* Hannah More was born in a little village, four miles outside Bristol.   Her father was the headmaster of the Fishponds Foundation School and Hannah, who at the age of three earned sixpence from the local rector for repeating her catechism, and at the age of four had composed a simple poem and was demanding writing paper in preference to toys, joined her four sisters in commencing a boarding school for girls in Bristol in 1758.

Bristol was a city of flourishing efficiency and a Mecca for successful merchants; it was therefore a centre for social life and the city sucked into its theatres, baths, and meeting places, nobility and titles without number.   Many of these found their way to the boarding school at 43 Park Street and thus increased its reputation.   Five lively, strong-minded ladies running a boarding school for young girls of the rich middle and upper classes took some contending with, and only people of strong personality entered the circle.   James Ferguson, the astronomer, and Thomas

(« Old Bubble and Squeak ») Sheridan, father of the famous playwright, came to lecture at the school.

When Hannah came to London to be courted by high society, she became a close friend of David and Mrs Garrick. David Garrick was the brilliant manager of a famous theatre in Drury Lane, the greatest living actor, and a playwright of significant ability. It is hardly surprising, therefore, that he was one of the most popular men in London society and Hannah frequently stayed at the Garrick's extravagant villa at Hampton. She walked the large well kept lawns that swept across the public highway and down to the Thames, and enjoyed the novelty of Garrick's tunnel that undermined that annoying highway. It was not long before Hannah herself was throwing parties for impressive lists of society folk. But in her hope for satisfaction here, she was deluded.

After the death of David Garrick in 1779, Hannah stayed with his wife until it was time to return to Bath where the sisters had opened a new school. But Bath was fast growing and noisy, and Hannah reacted by building a delightful cottage in Wrington, ten miles from Bristol. Here she began to be happy, writing poems, digging in her garden and entertaining the endless streams of influential visitors. In fact Hannah would have stayed here at « Cowslip Green » far longer but for the misfortune of having as a neighbour a slovenly farmer who, in addition to neglecting his fields, built pigsties close by where their sweet smell would most embarrass Hannah when the wealthy Henry Thornton and William Wilberforce visited her.

CARDIPHONIA

Ten years after her instant success, Hannah More became bored with the trivial round of society, and the hermitage at « Cowslip Green » gave her time for reflection.   In the year 1780 a copy of John Newton's recently published *Cardiphonia* came into her hands and began to mould her thinking.   It was not that Hannah was irreligious, she was a strong Church-woman and attended with Dr Johnson at his last communion service; all her plays and poems had a twist of moral teaching that was sincerely intended to reform manners.   But hers was the typically orthodox and fashionable faith of the day without bite or life.   The correspondence contained in *Cardiphonia* breathed the spirit of a religion of the heart and soul.   At the same time Hannah was coming into contact with the « Clapham Group » and their strong evangelical zeal impressed her immensely.

The poetess and playwright wrote a letter to the author of *Cardiphonia* and addressed the stranger in the familiar language of « My dear Sir ».   She received a response under « My dear Madam » and thus a long and close friendship grew up, mainly conducted by correspondence but supplemented by a visit to Cowslip Green in 1792.   Here Newton talked earnestly with Hannah More, walked and admired her garden, won the affection of the servants and absent-mindedly left his pipe lodged in a blackcurrant bush.   In 1787 Newton wrote that he understood perfectly her state of mind and longing for peace: « I have stood upon that ground myself, » he reassured her, and then urged her to wait upon the Lord: « For your encouragement—it is written, as in golden letters, over the gate of his mercy, Ask, and ye shall receive; Knock, and it shall be opened to you ». Hannah More had a wide correspondence and an even wider circle of friends, but it was from Newton that she principally sought advice for her soul, and through Wilberforce that she sought an outlet for her growing evangelical views. Hannah could hardly have been in more capable hands.

In 1789 Wilberforce visited « Cowslip Green » and completed his stay by a tour of the picturesque scenery of Cheddar, a pleasant village under the ridge of the Mendip Hills. On his return to the cottage in Wrington, Wilberforce commented : « Very fine, but the poverty and distress of the people are dreadful ». It was indeed dreadful. The inhabitants were a wild and lawless crowd, some actually living in caves and selling roots and stalactites to tourists to earn a living. But this scene of poverty, ignorance and the attendant evils could be multiplied all around, and Wilberforce planned the commencement of a Sunday School at Cheddar. He settled the issue with Hannah: « If you will be at the trouble, I will be at the expense ». The subsequent work cost Wilberforce and Thornton four hundred pounds a year.

CHEDDAR SUNDAY SCHOOLS
AND THE IMPORTANCE OF MANNERS

It was hard to convince the savage farmers of the benefits of educating the poor, and even harder to keep the children of the labourers coming. But Hannah, tramping the mud laden farm roads, was undeterred and tact and diplomacy for the one and a system of small bribes for the other (a penny for regular attendance and an occasional gingerbread treat) won the day. From this beginning a School of Industry was established to teach the girls spinning, weaving, knitting, and all the domestic arts so neglected in those desperately poor localities. A Sunday sermon was read (no extempore preaching for fear of riots at the charge of « methodist enthusiasm »). Womens' clubs were formed, and benefits handed out in the form of clothing.

In forty Somerset parishes Hannah righted the evil of the poor receiving short-weight bread. She wrote *The Cottage Book,* which contained sound advice to help the poor make the most of what they had, urging the men to plant wisely and the women to buy wisely. Within ten years sixteen villages had their own school and school teacher. Hannah wrote a series of *Penny Tracts,* which were entertaining stories, easy to read, close to the labourers' experience and full of moral, spiritual and political application. It was the time of the French Revolution, and the whiff of gunpowder and chopping of the guillotine were unpleasant sights and sounds so close to the English coastline.

This practical work of Hannah was the direct result of a radical change in her thinking, influenced largely by *Cardiphonia* and the personal correspondence of John Newton. Hannah's views of writing for the stage changed. She confessed to Newton her past views: « I was led to entertain what I must now think a delusive hope, that the stage, under certain regulations, might be converted into a school of virtue ». Later she wrote: « The fruits of the Spirit and the fruits of the stage, if the parallel were followed up, would exhibit as pointed a contrast as human imagination could conceive ». Mrs More, (in those days most maiden ladies had taken the courtesy title of « Mrs » by middle age), spent her time, and especially her Sundays, more carefully; she included in her reading « the more spiritual writers » among whom she named Baxter and, of course, Doddridge. By 1788 Hannah was ready to expose, more plainly than any of her plays or poems had done, the frivolous life of the rich. She published *Thoughts on the Importance of the Manners of the Great to General Society* and skilfully exposed those who acknowledged the truth of Christianity yet ended their thinking at the level of this world's goods. Hannah condemned the habit of employing hair-dressers on the Sabbath, and when Newton read this he could not forbid a smile as he recollected old William Wilson, the barber at Olney who, when he became a Baptist, refused to set Lady Austen's hair after Saturday evening and thus forced her to sit up all night to avoid disturbing it! But Hannah attacked all those little deceits that revealed the hypocrisy of society, like sending the servants to the door with « Not at home, Sir » to dismiss an unwanted visitor. She, who had attracted thousands to her plays, condemned Sunday theatres and concerts. Yet her language was so calm and gentle that even her old friends, who knew the attack to be so well directed, were not offended.

Hannah's attitude to charity had changed. She

240

condemned the view that considered « benevolence a substitute for Christianity », rather than the evidence for it. « It seems to be one of the reigning errors among some » she concluded, « to reduce all religion into benevolence, and all benevolence into alms-giving. » The book was warmly commended and even the Bishop of London claimed that it should find its way into every fine lady's library, and if not into her heart and manners, then the fault would be her own.

By 1811 Hannah More's books contained a more directly evangelical nature with such titles as *The Spirit of Prayer* and *Practical Piety, or the Influence of Religion of the Heart on the Conduct of Life.*

Four of the More sisters died within six years of each other, the first in 1813. Age and ill-health limited the remaining sister in her involvement in her previously vigorous work. She now lived in a large house at Barley Wood and outlived her last sister by fourteen years, dying in 1833 at the age of eighty nine. The good that Hannah More achieved by her Sunday Schools, tracts and books is incalculable. The influence upon all this by the quiet correspondence and friendship of John Newton cannot be over-estimated. Yet within one hundred years of a play that made her a mansion-hold name in the nation, Hannah More was all but forgotten.

TMD 16

CHAPTER 11

WAITING
FOR THE POST

In October 1788, just two years after Mary had set up her new home in Coleman Street, a light, airy location seven minutes' walk from the church, she called secretly upon a man who was an eminent surgeon in London, and a family friend. The following day, as John and Mary sat in the dining room exchanging news before the rector returned to his duties, Mary calmly spoke of her visit and of the surgeon's advice. Whilst they were living in Liverpool, Mary had received a severe blow on her chest, a small swelling appeared but was soon forgotten by them both. But the swelling grew, and when Mary visited the surgeon, he diagnosed a tumour which he compared to the size of half a melon. There was no possibility of his operating and he could advise nothing further than a peaceful life and rest. Not only was this virtually impossible in the busy Newton home, but during the severe winter of that year Betsy was taken seriously ill and John and Mary had much work in nursing her.

By the spring of 1789 Mrs Newton was rarely out of pain and the use of laudanum, which she hated, only slightly eased her discomfort. Mary could scarcely lie in bed for an hour at night and, as she tossed and turned, John's heart was torn with pity for her.   Much prayer was offered for Mary and by the summer she was able to visit Southampton with John and attended church once or twice.   But towards the end of the year her appetite went and the very sight or smell of meat was unbearable for her.   She retained a partiality for the small birds that were then delicate fare, and John later admitted: « At that time, I set more value upon a dozen larks, than upon the finest ox in Smithfield ».

Often during the day, between callers and calls, John would slip into her room and talk with Mary.   His eyes, that had seen so much human misery over the past sixty-four years, filled with tears, but a cheerful smile and comforting word from his wife settled his mind and when Sally came in to announce another caller, John was ready to return to his study and talk earnestly of the things of God.   Mary lay back and continued to read the hymns of Dr Watts, William Cowper and, of course, John Newton.

October 1790 was the most terrible time of all.   For two weeks Mary slumped into a depression and despair that changed her into another woman.   She feared death and would not allow it to be spoken of; she lost all hope of personal salvation and found no comfort in the Word of God; even to John, she spoke indifferently.   His heart was ready to burst, but he wisely adjudged the cause to be her illness.   It was a fleeting storm and Mary was soon composed and peaceful and delighting in the presence of her husband once more.

Mary's spine gave way and she could no longer move. She lay on her bed, spoke affectionately to John and squeezed his hand with hers, the only part of her body she could move without pain. John Thornton died one month before Mary and it was an added sorrow to them both.

The death of Mary.

On Sunday, December 12th, while John was preparing to leave for church, Mary called for him to say goodbye; John prayed, both cried and he went to his pulpit. When John returned Mary was still alive and conscious, and by waving her hand was able to assure him of her peace of mind. On Wednesday, at seven in the evening, Sally came to call Mr Newton into the bedroom. With a candle in his hand, John took up

245

his post by her bedside and watched for three hours.   The dim light cast his shadow across the room and turned him into a giant on the opposite wall.   A giant he was; a man devoted to the service of God now surrendering his last and dearest idol to his Lord.   On the 15th of December, 1790, a little before ten in the evening, Mary died and John gathered his servants around her bed, and poured out his heart in thankfulness to God.

« THE WORLD SEEMED TO DIE »

When Mary died, John later confessed: « the world seemed to die with her ».   Three days after the event he wrote to his old friend Bull: « I am supported, I am comforted, I am satisfied.   The Lord is good indeed!...   I trust we shall soon meet to part no more ».   That wish was not fulfilled, for John had seventeen years to run.   He regretted only one thing of their long and happy union, and that was that he had once made Mary his idol; even latterly he felt there had been too much of the golden calf in his love.

But now there was business at hand.   Had he not often told his congregation that a state of trial, if rightly improved, was, to the Christian, « a post of honour »?   Eyes were watching.   Would he exemplify his teaching?   Offers of help came from all quarters and John would have had no difficulty in filling his pulpit the following Sunday.   Nor did he, for on that day the congregation at St. Mary Woolnoth watched their own pastor mount the steps of the pulpit and give out his text from Habakkuk 3:17-18: « Although the fig tree shall not blossom, neither shall fruit be in the vines; the labour of the olive shall fail, and the fields shall yield no meat; the flock shall be cut off from the fold, and there shall be no herd in the stalls: yet I will rejoice in the Lord, I will joy in the God of my salvation ».

This was a passage he had never yet chosen as a text in his twenty-six years as a minister of the Gospel; he had long reserved it for this occasion, should he out-live Mary. The congregation rose to sing Newton's latest hymn based upon his text; in it he expressed what he now knew from experience:

> Domestic joys, alas, how rare!
>   Possess'd, and known by few!
> And they who know them, find they are
>   As frail and transient too.
>
> But you, who love the Saviour's voice,
>   And rest upon His name,
> Amidst these changes may rejoice,
>   For He is still the same.

It was a hymn of only eight verses. The poem John wrote for Mary on their twenty-fifth anniversary had contained twenty-one verses; however, a year after Mary had died he marked the occasion with thirty-eight! John reconciled himself to God's will, but never to Mary's absence; he could see her everywhere in the home. Unlike Cowper's absolute silence upon the name of Mary Unwin after her death, John never tired of referring to Mary Newton and the Lord's grace that sustained him through those terrible months of her illness.

THE ECLECTIC SOCIETY

In the year of Mary's death John was sent an honorary doctorate by the university of New Jersey, in America. He returned it with the courteous comment: « I am as one born out of due time. I have neither the pretension nor the wish to honours of this kind. However, therefore, the university may overrate my attainments, and thus show their respect, I must not forget myself; it would be both vain and improper were I to concur in it ». John Newton never allowed himself to forget that during the years when most young men were earning their degrees, he was a degraded slave tracing out geometry in the sand, on the Plantains of West Africa. A few letters arrived from Scotland which displeased him; he wrote to an old friend Mr Campbell: « I have been hurt by two or three letters directed to Dr Newton » and urged him to put the matter right with his friends in Scotland without delay: « I know no such person, I never shall, I never will, by the grace of God ».

But if John Newton had no desire for the preferments of the world, he was certainly concerned to be an able minister and to encourage his fellow ministers likewise. Whilst at Olney he had met frequently with local evangelical men whether dissenters or Churchmen, and almost as soon as he arrived in London he cast around to gather a similar band of men.

The Eclectic Society began in 1783 and a small group of evangelicals met, under the patronage of John Newton. Thomas Scott, who moved as chaplain to the Lock Hospital in that year, was one of the first members.   The rather scholastic title referred merely to the practice of sharing views on a chosen subject and thus helping one another to form a balanced opinion.   By 1791 it was felt wise to draw up a few rules.   John took up his small notebook and penned inside the stiff cover a summary of these rules agreed on May 26th.   They would meet at St. John's Chapel, a church in Bedford Row under the care of the Rev Richard Cecil, on a Monday and contribute one shilling, presumably to defray the cost of tea which was provided at half past four.   The chair was filled by each man in turn, and with « Bible on the Table », which John was careful to note, the meeting began.   The number of members was limited to thirteen and no-one was admitted if he lived beyond the five-mile stones around London.

John also kept a record of some of the subjects discussed, with occasional notes of points made.   The discussions were wide-ranging and practical: « What are the peculiar dangers of youth in the present day? » or, more appropriately for John: « How to make old age comfortable and honourable »; this was discussed on January 31st, 1791 when John felt old and alone without Mary.   On another occasion they discussed « How may we visit the sick to most advantage? ».   But elsewhere the subject was more doctrinal: « What is Christianity with or without the doctrine of the deity of Christ? »; « How to reconcile Paul and James on Justification », and « Who are the preachers of Free Grace, and who are the counterfeits? ».   In December 1795 they discussed that old problem that had nagged John when he first came to London: « How may we best introduce religious conversation in company? ».

John wrote three words below the title: « be gentle, gradual ». On April 9th, 1792 the subject was simply « On the slave trade ».

John considered this one of his most important meetings. He was never absent unless it was unavoidable and once had felt it necessary to explain to Mary that it was for her own good, and not for the Society meeting, that he had delayed setting out until the Tuesday to join her in Southampton. Even the Eclectic Society came second to Mary.

For all his fellowship with the dissenters, John Newton was a strong and convinced Churchman, yet not blind to the faults of his church or the Prayer Book. At certain points he regarded the Reformers as having « only made a beginning », and elsewhere he considered some of the fathers to be « old women in divinity ». He would neither accept nor use some phrases in the baptismal service, and particularly rejected the pronouncement, « this child is regenerate »; regeneration meant something far more to John Newton than sprinkling with water. He similarly rejected the view that those who die in infancy could only be saved if baptised: « I cannot think that the salvation of a soul depends upon a negligent or drunken minister, who cannot be found when wanted to baptise a dying infant ».

Soon after he arrived at Olney Newton had to bury one of his parishioners and wrote in his diary: « Ventured to omit a clause in one of the prayers, as I propose to do in such cases hereafter ». Doubtless the poor lady evidenced no saving faith and John was too honest slavishly to recite the hope that « when we shall depart this life, we may rest in him, *as our hope is this our sister doth* ».   This drew many charges upon his head, both from friend and foe.   But John was undeterred.   When men were contradicted by Scripture, experience and observation. whoever those men might be, he declared, « I pay little regard to their judgement ».

BETSY IN BEDLAM

With the death of his niece Eliza and his wife Mary, John turned naturally to Betsy Catlett for company.   At the age of thirty she tried hard to fill some of those gaps left by the loss of Mary.   She affectionately watched for his needs, walked with him when he took exercise and, as his eyesight began to fail, read to him also.   Betsy had brought a joy into the home for which Newton was always grateful.

The death of Eliza had filled Betsy Catlett with a morbid fear of death.   John counselled her, and to a large extent her fears disappeared over the next few years.   By 1801 she was contemplating marriage to an optician who owned a shop near the Royal Exchange and was also a member of St. Mary's, when her health broke down.   She suffered a nervous disorder so severe that John sadly commented that for two months she had been in the gloomy dungeon of Giant Despair.   Poor Betsy fell into such a disorder of mind that she was eventually committed to Bethlehem Hospital.   John had often been to this place, not for his

251

Sunday afternoon stroll as Cowper had done in his youthful days, but to preach to the inmates; the shepherd of Lombard Street had visited the London prisons for the same reason.

As early as 1775, during a visit to London, Newton was preaching at Bridewell, and in this prison, where earlier in the century the public would come to watch the women being flogged, he described his congregation as « housebreakers, highwaymen, pick-pockets, and poor unhappy women, such as infest the streets of the city, sunk in sin, and lost to shame ». On that day in September Newton had written to his maid Sally of the one hundred who sat, attentive to his message. He had given them the story of his own life and preached from 1 Timothy 1:15: « Christ Jesus came into the world to save sinners, of whom I am chief ». He confessed there were many tears in that place including his own. But that was not his last visit, and when he settled in London he went whenever he could, to preach to the patients and prisoners of hospital and prison, and once wrote that he was glad to be « out of Hell, out of Bedlam, out of Newgate ». Few who went to Bedlam came home again; if they were not mad when they arrived they very soon became so. Hope was abandoned here.

But John Newton did not abandon hope. Each day a servant walked with him to the end of Coleman Street where they would turn right at the London Wall; there he would wave and watch at Betsy's window until the answering white handkerchief was waved to and fro. Whatever the weather, John would never return home until that signal came. Newton was a man of stern discipline; a discipline he learned at sea.

Within a year Betsy had made a remarkable recovery and was tending the patients as best she could. To the immense joy of her uncle she was able to return home and in 1805 marry Mr Smith the optician. Husband and wife settled into number 6 Coleman Street where Betsy could continue to attend Newton's needs during the closing years of his life. « Heart-peace, house-peace, and church-peace », was how John described these latter years.

« LETTERS TO A WIFE »

Every year John and Betsy visited Southampton, where the only churches prepared to offer him the pulpit were dissenting chapels. He also toured the home counties, preaching and teaching. In 1793 John published *Letters to a Wife*. Some of his friends felt it almost unseemly that he should reveal, for all to read, the intimate correspondence received by Mary during his long sea journeys and during her subsequent separations from him. But Newton was unrepentant and felt that many would value his laying bare his heart in this way; in this assumption he was right.

One of the old rector's greatest loves was directed towards fellow ministers and particularly young men entering the church. As one familiar with poverty and hunger he would frequently send gifts to men whose cause was mentioned to him and a poor evangelical clergyman in Devon, who never met Newton, received many tokens of encouragement from the London minister. It was appropriate that when John Newton wrote a biography of Mr Grimshaw, a powerful preacher at Haworth, he donated the entire proceeds to the *Society for the Relief of Poor Pious Clergymen;* a society which commenced in 1788 with the enthusiastic support of Newton, and maintains a valuable work even today. His love for his household servants continued in London as it had at Olney. The servants grew old with their master and by 1793 John recognised that one young servant could have done the work of his three for « Phoebe is drooping, and I think will not hold out long; Crabb is very asthmatic; Sally but so-so ». Phoebe drooped quicker than Newton expected for she died the following day, after sixteen years' service. She was illiterate and ignorant, but found a warm place in Newton's heart and home.

On 30th March, 1800 Newton preached before the Lord Mayor and City authorities on the love of Christ. John was flattered by no-one and he plainly expounded his Gospel. His friendships had broadened and even Dr Johnson had become a close acquaintance before Johnson's death in 1784; the sculptor, John Bacon, had long been a close Christian friend and Newton began a correspondence with William Carey, the Baptist missionary in India.

THE OLD AFRICAN BLASPHEMER

At the age of seventy-six he was still preaching as loud, as long, and as often as before, and what is more, he was still being heard with acceptance. By the turn of his eightieth year he could manage only one service a month but was as punctual in time and as clear in his subject as ever. However, by the age of eighty Newton's sight was nearly gone; he could not join in much conversation and his memory began to fail. But still he preached on. At times he would leave his course, falter and have to be reminded of the point he had reached in his sermon; but his congregation did not diminish. He once apologised for not immediately recognising a visitor. « But I am very feeble », he excused himself, « I never experienced before what it was to be seventy-nine ».

Newton had many able curates during his time at St. Mary's and he could easily have given up. His friend, Richard Cecil, one day suggested that he should consider his work done « and stop before you evidently discover you can speak no longer ». The old man replied, raising his voice as if giving an order above the roar of the opposing sea: « I cannot stop. What, shall the old African blasphemer stop while he can speak? » Newton preached his last sermon in October 1806 in aid of a fund for the widows and orphans of Trafalgar. There could have been no occasion more fitting for the old sea captain.

John feared neither old age nor death. To one who enquired after his health he wrote that, through the divine favour he was perfectly well yet labouring under a growing disorder for which there is no cure: « I mean old age ». But he was glad of this disease: « For who would live always in such a world as this? ». Newton suffered occasional depressions but dismissed them as part of the symptoms of old age. To add to his sorrow, towards the turn of the century, his old friends began to « drop off like leaves in Autumn ». Death catches all men.

Newton delighted to counsel and advise young men entering the ministry, and they poured into his study. One of the last to receive spiritual counsel from the lips of the old African blasphemer was a young man about to sail on a missionary journey to India from which he would never return. Henry Martyn was twenty four years of age and within a few months he was due to leave England. This brilliant yet frail Cambridge graduate would speak eight languages, translate the New Testament into Hindustani, the New Testament and Psalms into Persian and many portions into Arabic before his untimely death, alone and friendless in the wastes of remote Turkey seven years later.

During the spring of 1805 Henry Martyn breakfasted with the venerable Newton. He was full of comfort and encouragement for the mind of the young missionary. Reminding Henry of the hard labour in God's service he spoke of a clever gardener, who claimed that he could sow his seeds whilst the meat was put on to roast and have the salad ready in time for the meal. « But », said the old man, « the Lord does not sow oaks in this way. » When Henry Martyn suggested he might never live to see the fruit of his proposed work, Newton answered that the missionary would have a bird's-eye view of it, which would be better. Martyn spoke of the opposition he would very likely meet with and drew from the old shepherd the response that he could not expect Satan to love him for the work he was about to do. Martyn concluded: « The old man prayed afterwards with sweet simplicity ».

The « old man » once assessed his purpose in life in this way: « I seem to see in this world two heaps, of human happiness and human misery: now if I can take but the smallest bit from one heap and add it to the other, I carry a point ».

On March 21st, 1805, John made his last entry in his journal. His eyes pained him as his shaking hand guided the pen uncertainly across the page. Yet the violence of that Atlantic storm fifty-seven years earlier was still vividly imprinted upon his mind. He must remember, as he had unfailingly done during the intervening years, the day when the light of heaven broke into his soul. The old man penned his final record: « Not well able to write; but I endeavour to observe the return of this day with humiliation, prayer, and praise ».

« WAITING FOR THE POST »

The eighteenth century was pre-occupied with death, and accounts of death-bed scenes and conversations were staple reading for the day. Whenever John Newton heard enquiry about the last expressions of an eminent believer he would respond: « Tell me not how the man died, but how he lived ». That has been done.

By January 1807, John Newton, whose sturdy legs once paced the decks of heaving ships, could no longer

257

walk.   By the following month he was confined to his bedroom but, with Betsy and her husband at hand to read to him, he found great comfort in the Word of God.   Towards the middle of the year John could not quickly recognise the voices of his closest friends, and the back that for Mary's sake was once torn with the lash, was bent and frail.

He spoke little, but when he did he was cheerful, and reassuring.   « I am », he said with a wrinkled smile, « like a person going a journey in a stage coach, who expects its arrival every hour, and is frequently looking out at the window for it ».   At another time he declared himself to be « packed and sealed, and waiting for the post ».

The spring flowers blossomed and died and the summer flitted past the bedroom window.   Visitors, timed and rationed by Betsy, came and went, greeting each other and exchanging the old man's condition in unnecessarily quiet tones.   In August the wonder of gas lighting was introduced into the streets of London; Beech and Whitecross Streets were illuminated and crowds gathered to stare at the brilliant and powerful lights.   Meanwhile, as the light of Newton's life came to a close and he waited for the last flicker to be extinguished, the weary old man exclaimed to his friends: « More light, more love, more liberty.   Hereafter I hope when I shut my eyes on the things of time I shall open them in a better world. »   He who had taken his vessel through many uncharted waters and had often been violently tossed by storm and gale added: « What a thing it is to live under the shadow of the wings of the Almighty ».   John Newton expressed himself unshaken in his faith and satisfied with the Lord's will. The leaves fell from the trees and scattered a carpet from Coleman Street to Lombard Street, but there was no pastor to walk that seven minutes to his pulpit. By December he confided in a friend: « My memory is nearly gone; but I remember two things: that I am a great sinner, and that Christ is a great Saviour ». On the evening of Monday, December 21st, 1807, John Newton died at the age of eighty-two.

John was buried at St. Mary Woolnoth beside Mary and Eliza. He had composed his own epitaph and requested that this and nothing else should be carved on a plain marble tablet; there was to be no other monument:

JOHN NEWTON

CLERK
ONCE AN INFIDEL AND LIBERTINE,
A SERVANT OF SLAVES IN AFRICA,
WAS,
BY THE RICH MERCY OF OUR LORD AND SAVIOUR

JESUS CHRIST,

PRESERVED, RESTORED, PARDONED,
AND APPOINTED TO PREACH THE FAITH
HE HAD LONG LABOURED TO DESTROY.

HE MINISTERED
NEAR XVI YEARS AS CURATE AND VICAR
OF *OLNEY* IN *BUCKS*
AND XXVIII AS RECTOR
OF THESE UNITED PARISHES

ON FEBRY THE FIRST MDCCL HE MARRIED

MARY

DAUGHTER OF THE LATE GEORGE CATLETT,
OF *CHATHAM KENT,*
WHOM HE RESIGNED
TO THE LORD WHO GAVE HER,
ON DECR THE XVTH MDCCXC.

In the year that the candles flickered out in some of the London streets and the brilliance of gas began to spread slowly across the city, John Newton died; a small trembling light extinguished. But the flame of his ministry in pulpit, example, correspondence, and hymns has never ceased to illuminate the people of God even two hundred and fifty years after his birth.

INDEX

Africa (see also West Africa) 37, 38, 42, 51, 112, 194, 211
African 87, 93, 94, 98
Alicante 11
America 37, 102, 105, 161, 217, 233, 248
A Monument to the Praise of Eliza Cunningham 215
An Authentic Narrative 135-136, 172, 210, 217, 219, 225
An Ecclesiastical History 138
Anne, Queen 103, 104
Antigua 94
Apologia 213
Arminians 212
Atkins, John 40, 52
Austen, Lady 185, 240

Bacon, John 254
Baptists 114, 152, 220, 240, 254
Bars 84
Bath 236
Baxter, Richard 240
Bedford 121
Bee 98, 100, 101
Berkhamsted 166
Bethlehem Hospital (Bedlam) 166-167, 251-252
Bible Society 233
Bradbury Rev « Bold » 103, 152
Brewer, Rev. Samuel 101, 102, 108
Bridewell, prison 252
Brighton 216
Bristol 105, 235, 236
H.M.S. Britannia 25
Browne, Moses 128
Brownlow 68-73, 89, 112
Buchanan, Claudius 218-219
Buckingham, Duchess of 102
Buckinghamshire 119
Bull, William 153-154, 185, 216, 246

Calvinism 110, 151, 212
Cambuslang 218
Canterbury, Archbishop of 140
Cape Lopez 54-55
Cardiphonia 138, 154, 210, 237, 239
Carey William 158-159, 220, 254
Carteret, Captain Philip 9, 18, 19, 36, 45
Carteret, Lord 24
Catlett, Elizabeth (Betsy) 140, 194, 214, 243, 251-253, 258
Catlett, George 15, 140
Catlett, Jack 15, 24, 75, 85, 118
Catlett, Mr. and Mrs. 15, 24, 68, 69, 100
Cecil, Lord David 191
Cecil, Richard 132, 249, 255
Characteristics of Men, Manners, Opinions, Times etc. 13-14
Charles II, King 42
Charles Town 75
Charlies 193
Chatham 15, 23-25, 29, 45, 67-68, 75-77, 100, 101, 124, 130
Cheddar 238
Chester, Bishop of 116, 120
Church Missionary Society 233
Church of England 102, 120, 155, 213, 233
Clapham Group 233, 237
Clow 41-50, 70, 83
Clunie, Alexander 97-98, 101, 134, 150
Coleridge 64
Common Prayer, Book of 90, 250
Consumption 214-215
Conyers, Dr. 173
Cornwallis, General 163
Cotton, Dr. Nathaniel 171

261

265

INDEX OF SCRIPTURE REFERENCES

INDEX OF FIRST LINE OF HYMNS

BIBLIOGRAPHY

General

Title	Author	Publisher and Date
London in the Eighteenth Century	Sir Walter Besant	A and C Black, 1925
The Age of Illusion	James Laver	Weidenfeld and Nicolson 1972
The Georgians at Home	Elizabeth Burton	Longmans, 1967
The Whig Supremacy	Basil Wilkins	Oxford, 1962
Wesley's England	J.H. Whiteley	Epworth, 1938
The British Seaman	Christopher Lloyd	Collins, 1968
Jack Tar	John Laffin	Cassell, 1969
The Merchantmen	Richard Armstrong	Ernest Benn, 1969
History of the Liverpool Privateers with an account of the Liverpool Slave Trade	Gomer Williams	Frank Cass and Co, 1966 (original 1897)
Liverpool and the Mersey	F.E. Hyde	David and Charles, 1971
The Rise of the Port of Liverpool	Parkinson	Liverpool University Press, 1952
A History of Sierra Leone	A.P. Kup	Cambridge University Press, 1961
Sierra Leone - A Modern Portrait	Roy Lewis	Her Majesty's Stationery Office, 1958
A Voyage to Guinea, Brazil and the West Indies	John Atkins	Frank Cass, 1970 (original 1735)
Shaftesbury's Characteristics	ed. J.M. Robertson	Grant Richards, 1900
The Life of God in the Soul of Man	Henry Scougal	Inter Varsity Press, 1961
Rise and Progress of Religion in the Soul	P. Doddridge	Religious Tract Society, 1892

Biography

Title	Author	Publisher and Date
William Wilberforce	Travers Buxton	Religious Tract Society
The Life of William Wilberforce (5 volumes)	Robert and Samuel Wilberforce	John Murray, 1838
Thomas Scott the Commentator	A.C. Downer	Charles Thynne, 1909
The Life of the Rev. Thomas Scott	John Scott	Seeley and Burnside, 1836
Hannah More	Helen Knight	American Tract Society, 1862
Hannah More	Mary Hopkins	Longmans Green and Co, 1947
Henry Thornton of Clapham	Standish Meacham	Harvard University Press, 1964
Life of Col. James Gardiner	P. Doddridge	Religious Tract Society
Memoirs of Buchanan	Hugh Pearson	Seeley and Burnside, 1834
Life of Joseph Milner	Isaac Milner	Religious Tract Society
A Memoir of the Rev. Henry Martyn	John Sargent	Seeley, Jackson and Halliday, 1855
William Carey	S. Pearce Carey	Hodder and Stoughton, 1923
The Dictionary of National Biography	ed. Sir Leslie Stephens and Sir Sidney Lee	Oxford University Press
The Town of Cowper	Thomas Wright	Sampson Low, Marston and Co. 1893
Cowper - Verse and Letters	ed. Brian Spiller	Rupert Hart-Davis, 1968
Cowper's Works	ed. Rev. T.S. Grimshawe	W. Nimmo, 1875
The Life of William Cowper	Thomas Wright	C.J. Farncombe and Sons Ltd, 1921
Life and Works of Cowper	ed. William Hayley	W. Tegg and Co, 1847
The Stricken Deer	Lord David Cecil	Constable, 1933

268

John Newton

Title	Author	Publisher and Date
John Newton. Out of the Depths	Autobiography	First published, 1764
John Newton	Josiah Bull	Religious Tract Society
Memoirs of the Rev. John Newton	Richard Cecil	J. Hatchard, 3rd edition, 1808
The Life of John Newton	Based on autobiography and letters	Seeley Jackson and Halliday, 1855
Amazing Grace	Demaray	Light and Life Press, 1958
An Ancient Mariner	Bernard Martin	Wyvern, 1962
The Journal of a Slave Trader 1750-54	Bernard Martin and Mark Spurrell	Epworth, 1962
Six Discourses as Intended for the Pulpit		First published Liverpool 1760
Letters to a Wife		First published London 1793
Omicron		First published Olney 1774
Cardiphonia		First published London 1780
Letters of John Newton	Josiah Bull	Religious Tract Society
Olney Hymns		First published Olney 1779

Unpublished Material (quoted or referred to)

	Source
Letter to ' Dear Bet. ' re 1780 Gordon Riots	Guildhall Manuscript Library, London
Letters to Rev. Thomas Scott	Guildhall Manuscript Library, London
Poor Law Rate Books of Chatham	Rochester Museum, Kent
Captain's Log for H.M.S. Harwich 1744-1745	Public Records Office, London
First Lt. Ruffin's Log and other lieutenants' Logs H.M.S. Harwich 1744-45	National Maritime Museum, Greenwich

Some Significant dates in the Life of John Newton

July 24th 1725	Born
February 25th 1744	Impressed onto H.M.S. Harwich
March 10th 1748	Violent storm led to his first prayer for years
March 21st 1748	Newton's conversion
February 1st 1750	Married to Mary Catlett
August 11th 1750	First command as Master of the Duke of Argyle
August 19th 1755	Tide Surveyor at Liverpool
September 14th 1755	Lunch with Whitefield
April 29th 1764	Ordained into Deacon's orders
May 27th 1764	First Sermon as Curate-in-Charge, Olney
August 14th 1767	Cowper's first stay at the Vicarage
August 12th 1773	Cowper's second stay at the Vicarage
December 19th 1779	First sermon as Rector of St Mary Woolnoth
December 7th 1785	First counselled Wilberforce
December 15th 1790	Death of Mary
March 21st 1805	Final entry into his journal
December 21st 1807	Died.